## — *Mike Bowman* —

# The
# Ds
## of the
# Deal

**18 Principles That Build Cash and Equity in Real Estate and Real-Life Situations**

*Not in my wildest dreams did I think my wife and I would have a million-dollar apartment complex by age 23.*

**Ds of the Deal:**

**18 Principles That Build Cash and Equity in Real Estate and Real-Life Situations**

Copyright © 2020 by Mike Bowman

All rights reserved, including the right to reproduce this book or portions thereof in any form whatsoever without the written permission of the copyright holder.

ISBN-13: 979-8567324837

Photos provided by Mike Bowman.

Editing by WordEthic, LLC.

Visit WordEthic for information.

WordEthic
YOU'RE ONLY AS GOOD AS YOUR WORDS

**Ds of the Deal is dedicated to Randy Ott.**

"Not in my wildest dreams did I think my wife and I would have a million-dollar apartment complex by age 23."

*Mike Bowman*

**Ds of the Deal** ─────────────────

# Table of Contents

Something About Me ........................................... v

Let's Get Started .............................................. xi

D 1 - Death .................................................... 1

D 2 - Divorce ................................................ 31

D 3 - Disease ................................................ 37

D 4 - Desperate ............................................. 41

D 5 - Debt .................................................... 50

D 6 - Dated ................................................... 59

D 7 - Dumb ................................................... 69

D 8 - Dumpy ................................................. 81

D 9 - Disaster ............................................... 86

D 10 – Dropped Out of Contract ..................... 92

**Ds of the Deal**

D 11 - Done ..................................................98

D 12 - Decline.............................................103

D 13 - Depression ......................................108

D 14 - Drunk ..............................................112

D 15 - Demand ..........................................118

D 16 - Desire..............................................135

D 17 – Dirtbag (Don't Be One) ......................145

D 18 – Ds of the Deal Capital .......................147

Final Deal..................................................150

Leave a Review ..........................................153

www.mcgeebowman.murney.com

**Ds of the Deal**

# Something About Me

If you and I do not yet know each other, it is important for you to understand I am possibly one of the cheapest people you ever will meet. I've picked up pennies, nickels, dimes and quarters off the ground for as long as I can remember. I am *very* money minded, and think having a money mindset is a blessing.

At times though, my intense money mindset does feel a little extreme. Let me give just one example. My wife and I were newly married and loving life, but like even the most loving couples, we had some adjustments to make because we had never been around each other 24/7.

During those early months of our marriage, I was penny-pinching. Not only would I run across a parking lot to pick up a penny, but I tried to save money everywhere I could to have more funds for Britney's and my future fortunes and planned investments in real estate.

# Ds of the Deal

One of my pet peeves was using the air conditioners in our cars. I knew that running the A/C reduced gas mileage and that you could save a few dollars per tank if you didn't use it. In my mind, that was a stellar idea, a great epiphany. I would do almost anything to save a couple of bucks, including riding in a hot, sweaty car during the summer. I implemented this A/C boycott and confirmed I was getting slightly better gas mileage.

Convinced, I decided to force my wife to follow suit. I got onto her all the time for using the A/C in her car, and continually pushed her to just roll down her windows instead. Imagine being married to me at that time. Not many women would have made it. Lol.

One night, I had just finished a rough day at work, and so had Britney. We headed to her dad's house to spend a little time with him.

After hanging out for a while, we decided to head home. I jumped in the driver's seat of Britney's car, turned the ignition and turned off the A/C. Britney jumped in the front passenger seat and turned the A/C back on. I, of course, gave Britney a look and turned the A/C back off.

We started driving and only got about halfway through the neighborhood before Britney turned

# Ds of the Deal

the A/C back on. We started to argue and some harsh words were said. To my surprise, Britney opened the door and got out of the moving car. We were going less than five miles an hour through the neighborhood, but still, I was shocked.

Britney walked back to her dad's house. I was left with two decisions. I could head home without Britney and have an even angrier wife, or I could go back to my father-in-law's house and let her use all the A/C she wanted on the way home. I'm ashamed to admit that was a tough question for me at the time.

I really thought about just going home and fighting with my wife because she wasn't as motivated to save money as me. Against that instinct, I bucked up and went back to try and resolve the conflict. I showed up, we called an uneasy truce, and drove home with the A/C blowing cold.

Since that day, I've learned to love air conditioning.

Looking back, I see I was acting a little crazy, or insane as my wife could have described me. Now, I blast air conditioning in my new Toyota Tacoma almost everywhere I go during the warmer months. I have a different mindset now, a mindset more about finding a healthy balance between saving and earning and spending. You can't save your way toward wealth or freedom, although saving along the way does help.

I was not always this way. I was not always as frugal, business-minded, and driven as I am today. I remember a day, really not too many days ago, in sixth grade, sitting on my best friend's bunk-bed, stoned, eating Chinese food and watching cartoons.

## Ds of the Deal

Much has happened since that day in sixth grade. I often hear motivational speakers say, "if I can do it, anyone can do it." As cheesy as that claim may be, it is perfectly true in my situation.

If I could go from getting stoned as a sixth-grader on a buddy's bunk-bed to closing multi-million-dollar Deals, giving my family a prosperous lifestyle, driving a brand new Toyota Tacoma, then you can, too.

This book can help.

## Ds of the Deal

The world is here for the taking, for anyone who applies the *Ds of the Deal* and the principles of *HUSTLE Then Repeat*. Those who apply these crucial principles will find similar success—helping others get what they want—if that is what you desire.

**Ds of the Deal**

# Let's Get Started

If you and I are alike, and I believe we are, you are looking to get good Deals. Good Deals come in many forms and in many ways. In this book, we will discuss just a few of the ways you can get the good Deals you so greatly desire. As we learned in *HUSTLE Then Repeat*, it can be fun and effective to think outside the box and put together extraordinary Deals.

Today, right now, while you are reading or listening to this book, you and I will explore a few added avenues that can bring you good Deals and success as you see it. Together, we will discuss what I have come to call the Ds of the Deal. They are eighteen principles, each starting with the letter D, that will lead you to good Deals and provide opportunities for you to build up cash and equity.

The more cash and equity I build up in my business, the more and more fun it gets. Bigger numbers equal bigger fun. Bigger numbers equal bigger risks and equally higher rewards.

## Ds of the Deal

I encourage you to read or reread *HUSTLE Then Repeat* alongside this book. They go hand-in-hand when it comes to finding and securing the best Deals possible, the best way to provide solutions to other people's problems.

**Ds of the Deal**

# D 1 - Death

*No one wants to die. Even people who want to go to heaven don't want to die to get there. And yet death is the destination we all share. No one has ever escaped it. And that is as it should be, because death is very likely the single best invention of life. It is life's change agent. It clears out the old to make way for the new.*

**Steve Jobs**

If there's one thing you and I and every other person on this planet is guaranteed, it is Death. Death will happen to every person who walks this world. That's a fact. Death is something sacred, not something to be talked about lightly. You likely have known someone who has died in your family, extended family, friend group, circle of influence, or workplace. Death is a factor of life.

Denzel Washington once said, "You'll never see a U-Haul behind a hearse."

# Ds of the Deal

There is a point beyond the humor. Everything you own will be left on this world when you depart through Death. This means all your assets, a home or real estate, vehicles, stocks, trades, bonds, precious metals, all will be left to your successors. Your successors then have the opportunity to keep or to sell your assets. Most successors sell the assets of the deceased.

Death, as unfortunate as it is, can be a great opportunity for you and others like you to get good Deals, good for you and good for the successor. As one primary purpose of this book is for you to find good Deals, it is important to know that Death will sometimes bring you opportunities. Death has brought me more good Deals than any other cause, some of my best Deals.

Note that I'm not encouraging you to hassle helpless widows, or wait around at hospitals for people to keel over. Be mindful of every business situation you encounter.

You can be the best solution for someone in need, and at the same time create a win-win scenario because you are benefiting from the Deal, as well. Your lowball offer may be the best exit strategy for a potential seller, not necessarily because of the purchase price, but more because

## Ds of the Deal

of the quick purchase and walk-away situation for the successor/seller.

Although you can get good Deals through a Death, never take unfair advantage of any person. People need to consent to these Deals when you put them together.

Let me share with you a few examples of why a Death may be cause for a good Deal.

### The Delmar House

As you might remember from *HUSTLE Then Repeat*, I frequently make lowball offers on newly listed properties for sale in my geographical area. These are always lowball offers, always cash, close quickly, as is, no seller repairs, no contingencies, no inspections. This makes it easier for the seller.

While making my routinely lowball offers one day, I stumbled across a house on Delmar Street. side of town, but was not in the same neighborhood as the doctors and lawyers. This home and neighborhood could be classified as decent or normal.

This was a 3-bedroom, 1-bathroom, 1000-square-foot home that needed a complete remodel. When I saw the pictures of the decaying wood siding, massively stained carpets, wet ceilings from a bad roof, and overgrown yard, I knew this was exactly the type of home I needed to purchase.

I learned early in my investing career that the crappier the house, the more money there was to be made on it. This is true because the crappier the house, the cheaper the purchase price.

You have the opportunity to put sweat equity, or earned equity, into the home by fixing it up.

## Ds of the Deal

Seeing as this home was in need of some extreme love, I decided to make an offer right on the spot, while staring at the pictures of this crappy home on my office computer. I had yet to see the house in person, all I had seen was pictures on the online listing. But I knew the location, did a rough estimate of repairs in my brain, and put together a ridiculous offer that I was sure the seller would never accept.

With this home being listed for almost $40k, I decided a no-brainer purchase price would be $10k. Can you believe that, lowballing just 25 percent of the asking price? Most people don't have the guts or the nuts to do something so potentially offensive. I, on the other hand, don't give a crap about what anybody thinks. Luckily, I have been blessed with and have nurtured a high self-esteem, so what people think of me is usually one of the last things on my mind.

So, sight unseen, I called the listing realtor to make my $10k offer. Throughout my conversation with the listing realtor, while noting a few pieces of information on the pages of the seller's disclosures, I realized that the seller had inherited the property within the last few weeks.

As bad as it may sound, this was music to my ears. Usually, when a person inherits a piece of property, or anything of value, they are more willing to let it go at a lower price. This is true because the successor of the deceased, the person who inherited the asset, did not put any money into it and has no skin in the game. There's a different thought process when you are selling something that you have worked hard for or taken many years to pay off or put blood, sweat, and tears into, as opposed to something you got for free that you never had to work for or contribute to.

This scenario is even sweeter for the buyer when there is a multiple sibling effect, meaning

## Ds of the Deal

that the more successors involved, the more likely you are to get a possible Deal. More than likely, the siblings are uninterested in or fed up with the asset. More than likely after the proceeds of sale, each sibling isn't even taking home that much money. Many siblings would rather just get it over with as soon as possible regardless of a lower purchase price.

As soon as I learned the seller of the Delmar house had recently inherited the property, I was even more confident I could get a Deal. I was sure I could push my lowball offer of cash, as is, no contingencies, and get the good Deal I wanted and needed.

It is important to understand that often an inherited piece of property or asset is paid off, meaning there is little or no loan attached to said asset. Because there is no payoff on the property or asset, there is no precise dollar amount that needs to be received to cover any previous debt of the deceased. This allows the successor to let the property or asset go at less than accessed value.

After submitting my lowball $10k offer, the seller's realtor called back to say the seller would do $20k. I stayed firm at $10k. The seller came back with another counter offer, asking if I would do $15k. Again, I stuck to my guns and did not

# Ds of the Deal

budge from my $10k offer. I was a little surprised that counter offers were being thrown my way, but was even more surprised that the seller hadn't just rejected my interest right off the bat. To make the Deal sweeter, I allowed the listing realtor to represent me as buyer, as well as continue to represent the seller. This means that the seller's realtor just got a *pay raise*. She would now not only make the commission for the listing side, but also could make a double commission by representing me on the buying side.

After making this fact and my other appealing terms of the offer very clear, the seller said they would accept my $10k offer. I quickly got my offer on paper and emailed it to the listing agent for her seller to sign. I always recommend giving the whole commission for the sale to the person representing the seller. This motivates the realtor to *get things done*. His or her paycheck doubles because they are representing both sides of the Deal instead of one.

How would you feel if your paycheck doubled overnight? Good feeling, right? What would you do for a double paycheck?

If no realtor is involved, obviously there would be no commission to give or take. It is also very appealing to most sellers when you pay their

## Ds of the Deal

closing costs. Closing cost is a broad term that describes the transfer fees of a property.

Usually a transfer of ownership occurs at a title company, where there are closing fees, closing protection letters, e-filing of documents such as the warranty deed, and a few other things in that same realm of expertise. Title company costs usually run about $600 per side of the transaction, meaning that the buyer pays about $600 in closing costs and the seller pays about $600 in closing costs.

I find it is very enticing when you offer to pay the seller's closing costs. Paying the seller's closing costs is just one less thing for them to worry about, and doesn't cost you that much more money. It may actually get you a lower purchase price on the property that more than compensates for the seller closing costs.

Within a few hours of submitting my written offer of $10k to the seller's realtor, I received the signed contract back and was overjoyed. I couldn't believe someone would let that house go for only $10k. You probably drive a car that's more expensive than that home.

Within a few hours of signing my $10k offer, the seller received a higher offer that would have certainly put more money in her pocket. Of course, since she had already signed my legal offer, she was bound to our $10k Deal.

Knowing that someone else was willing to pay more than I did reassured me that I had, in fact, gotten a great Deal on this little house.

This house needed about $28k worth of immediate updates and repairs, new flooring, fresh paint, a complete bathroom gut and remodel, new windows, new siding, new roof, new central HVAC, new gas lines, foundation repair, new soffit and facia, sealed front porch, updated electrical, and major lawn care.

After these much-needed repairs and updates, this home was sure to be worth almost $100k.

## Ds of the Deal

As it turned out, after it was completely fixed up, every update completed, the property appraised at $98k when Britney and I went to refinance, the refinance that we always do after completing a renovation project as stated in the BRRRR—Buy, Remodel, Rent, Refinance, Repeat—Method.

What a great day that was, as it's always a good day when you have an appraisal come in as you anticipated or even a little higher. It was because Britney and I bought this house so cheap that we were able to profit in the end. It is because we were the solution to someone's problem—a lady who had recently inherited property because of the death of her father—that we were able to profit. This was definitely a win-win situation. The seller of the Delmar house got the money she needed, and Britney and I were able to keep occupied with this project and create equity that was not there before.

If you learn nothing else from this book, learn this principle:

*You make your money when you buy.*

### The Woodland House

As bad as it may sound, my best Deals have come from a Death/inheritance situation. The Woodland house was one of my most profitable Deals up until then.

The Woodland house is a 2-story, 2,300-square-foot, 4-bedroom, 2-bathroom, 2-car garage home with a nice bonus room—or nonconforming 5th bedroom—upstairs for the kids to play in.

This Woodland house was conveniently located near the mall, hospitals, and many other restaurants and conveniences on the southern, wealthier side of town.

## Ds of the Deal

This home, like almost every home Britney and I purchased, needed everything: new siding, new soffit/facia, new windows, new flooring, fresh paint, new fixtures, updated electrical, a massive amount of lawn work.

It also needed a complete clean out as the trash was almost to the ceiling in some places.

Let me tell you how I became acquainted with the Woodland house, and how I was given the option to purchase it. It was a pretty normal day, and my wife and I were finishing our latest rental remodel on another property. Since we were

## Ds of the Deal

about to wrap up our current project, we needed something else in the pipeline for the coming weeks and months to keep our rental game going and further our business. I decided to call a local wholesaler from whom I'd bought a property or two.

A property wholesaler buys homes cheap and sells them AS IS, usually without doing any repairs or even touching the home, for a higher price to other investors. This wholesaler is a master of the Ds of the Deal, skilled at finding people in these unfortunate situations who need a way out.

Because of his skill at putting Deals together with unfortunate people in need of a best-case scenario, I gave him a ring and asked what he currently was wholesaling.

Luckily enough, he mentioned a two-story house on Woodland Street that needed a complete gut and remodel. I met him over at the home immediately, to crunch my numbers and run an assessment of what repairs the home needed, and how much it would cost.

When I asked for some background, the wholesaler said this home was owned by a little old lady who had recently passed away. Her kids

# Ds of the Deal

inherited the property directly from her, which got me even more excited.

Because this Death led to an inheritance, my wholesaling buddy was able to secure the home at a very low price, which meant he was able to wholesale it to me for a low price.

Let's use some easy numbers as an example. Let's say my wholesaler friend bought this home worth $130k, even in bad condition, for $50k from the kids who inherited it from their mother after her passing. Let's also say that wholesaler in turn sold the home to me for $70k.

Even though I bought the property for $20k more than what my wholesaler paid, we were all still winners. The kids who inherited the property were winners because they got a cash offer, unloading a potential burden, a big house needing expensive repairs. My wholesaler buddy was a winner because he bought a house for $50k and sold it for $70k the same day, without doing a single repair. I was a winner because I bought a home for $70k that's worth $130k. Everyone was a winner, everyone got a slice of the pie. That's exactly what happened.

Because of a Death, my wholesaler buddy was able to purchase the home at a low enough purchase price to still make money on it and give

**Ds of the Deal**

me a good Deal. It was a win-win for everyone involved, including the kids who consented to accept the $50k offer for the Woodland house.

After purchasing the Woodland house, I made it brand new again. We did every single thing needed, from replacing the roof and windows and siding down to cleaning the sinks in the bathroom and installing new toilets.

After our glorious remodel was complete, we had spent about $30k, and had taken six weeks to do it. After adding my purchase price of $70k and remodel cost of $30k, I had $100k invested. After repairs, the house appraised for $165k.

## Ds of the Deal

Can you believe that? We made $65k equity in just six weeks. That is like making $10,833.33 a week for six weeks straight.

That's great money, a great Deal, caused by a Death/inheritance, where everyone benefited. This Deal wouldn't have been so sweet if the initial purchase price had been higher. If this home had been listed on the open market for everyone and their brother and their dog to bid on, I have no doubt it would've sold for $130k before repairs.

# Ds of the Deal

Let's play with the scenario a bit and say you would have not found this home from a wholesaler from kids who inherited the property. Let's say you bought this home listed for $130k on the open market. After your $30k for needed repairs, you would have invested $160k in a property that was only worth $165k. See the difference?

You always make your money when you buy, and you can buy a whole lot cheaper when a property is inherited following a Death.

Again, the purpose of this chapter in *The Ds of the Deal* is not to harass people who have problems or are currently going through difficulties, or have recently lost a loved one.

What I am imploring you to do is to be a solution to someone's problem. Be their best-case scenario at the moment. Be their walk-away offer, where all they need to do is walk away and receive their cash offer, hassle free. The Woodland house was a slam dunk. The equity my wife and I gained was immense, and we were actually able to secure a loan/refinance after the remodel on the home in accordance with the BRRRR Method.

After all was said and done, we took this Woodland rental home to our local bank and got a

# Ds of the Deal

loan on the property for 80 percent of the $165k appraised value. The bank loaned us $132k on a home where we had only $100k invested.

These are the type of Deals you want, Deals that will not only be 100 percent funded, but have money left over at the end of the day to put toward your next property remodel or investment.

## The Fort House

Britney and I called that same local wholesaler and asked what other Deals he had available. He mentioned there was a home on Fort they had recently purchased from a kid. By "kid" he meant a gentleman of 30 or 40 who inherited a home from his father who had recently passed away.

I hurried over to this 3-bedroom, 2-bathroom, 2-car garage, 1200-square-foot home to give it a good look over and see what needed to be done.

This home was actually in livable shape as it sat. The thick green shag carpet, green bathroom vanity, green bathroom tub, and green bathroom flooring all were well-maintained, despite its Datedness.

If we emptied the contents of the home, and gave the carpets a good clean, I felt fairly certain we could move a tenant in right away.

**Ds of the Deal**

But, I knew there was an even better way.

The better way was to buy the house cheap, make it brand new by installing new flooring, fresh paint, new electrical, new windows, new siding, new soffit, new facia, new gutters, and other odds and ends, then refinance it like always using the BRRRR Method.

## Ds of the Deal

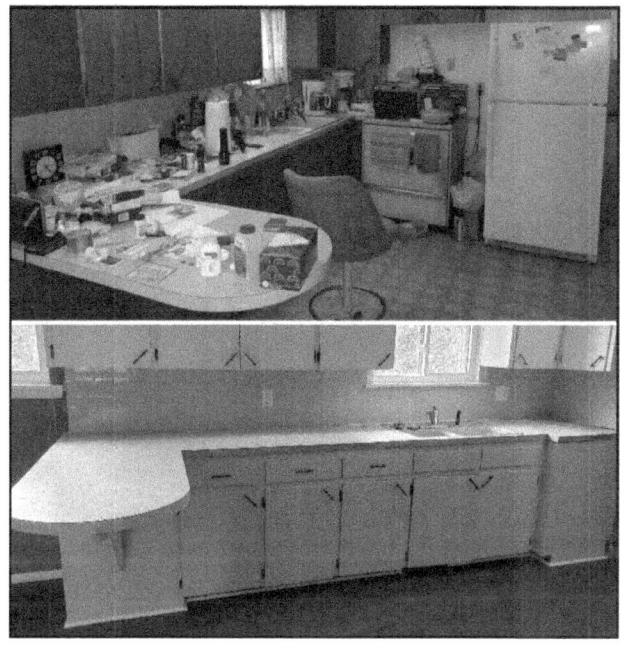

My wholesaler buddy had gotten the home for about $40k from this kid who inherited the property. I got the home cheap—about $50k—from my wholesaling buddy.

With $50k invested in the wholesale price and another $20k invested in the four-week remodel, Britney and I had $70k invested in the property.

**Ds of the Deal**

Once finished, the property appraised at $115k, meaning the bank was willing to loan us 80 percent of the appraised value, or $90k. Another slam dunk, another good Deal provided by an inheritance following a Death.

With our monthly bank payment on a 10-year note being $900, we rented out the home shortly after the remodel for $920 a month. Britney and I set up a lot of our early loans on 10-year terms, as opposed to a 20- or a 25-year term, to get them paid off as soon as possible as opposed to

# Ds of the Deal

paying them off later and eventually paying more interest.

Our goal with our first properties in our early bank loans was too get them paid off as soon as possible. Find out what your goal is, where you want to be in 10 or 15 or 20 years, and start laying the foundation for that dream today.

## The Airwood House

Many good Deals tend to start with the question, "What else you got?"

Deals are all around, you just have to find them. Many people are willing to sell low or give stuff away, so you need to find them and be the first solution to their problem. A perfect situation that demonstrated these good Deals all around was the South Airwood Deal.

One morning, as I was going through the new property listings—new properties that have been listed for sale—I stumbled across a 3-bedroom, 2-bathroom, 2-car garage home on the good side of town that looked like it needed a little love. I called the listing realtor, made a lowball offer, as always, just to get rejected, as usual.

When the listing agent was about to hang up, I asked him the crucial question: "What else you got?"

He gladly responded, "I have a home on Airwood that might be more your caliber."

After talking about this 3-bedroom, 2,-bathroom, 2-car garage, 1,200-square-foot home on Airwood, I learned this realtor was actually the property owner. His mom had recently died, leaving a few rental properties to her son as an inheritance, this listing realtor. Seeing the opportunity to swoop in and pick up this neglected little rental house, I decided to make a low cash offer. The seller started at $75k, and I started at $50k.

Over the next few weeks, I stayed persistent in the negotiation for this rental home. We finally settled on the purchase price of $65k. It was a more than fair Deal, and I was pleased. This particular home only needed about $20k in

# Ds of the Deal

remodel costs, which took eight weeks. By the end, Britney and I had $85k in this newly revamped rental home.

The appraisal came in at $115k, so we created $30k of equity in just eight weeks, which averages out to $3,750 a week in equity gained.

I hope you don't think of these examples as us boasting. It really isn't. I am just showing you how you can gain success, too.

Anyone can attain the success they desire, especially when they find out the formula to do it.

Part of the success formula is being the solution to post-death/inheritance problems.

## Ds of the Deal

**The Kissimmee House**

As unfortunate as it may be, a Death has led to many good Deals, such as the Deal for Britney and me to purchase a house on Kissimmee Street.

A little backstory: this home was not even for sale. I didn't know it existed. While leaving my shared real estate office, I struck some ordinary conversation with another realtor who shares the office.

After our normal conversation, I asked: "Got any good Deals up your sleeve?" To my surprise, this fellow realtor said he did have a good Deal and was willing to share the details with me.

Those age old questions—"Got any Deals up your sleeve?" "What else you got?" "Anything else?"—have made all the difference in my business growth.

Many good Deals have come from asking a simple question that leads to a potential property or product.

This was a 4-bedroom, 2-bathroom, 2-story, 2-car garage home in a fairly desirable neighborhood, but as so often is the case, the house needed some updating and love.

**Ds of the Deal**

I, of course, was willing to do the updating and give the love this property needed, as long as the price was right.

You will find that everything is worth something, even if it's only two or three dollars. A wrecked motorcycle isn't completely finished, you just need to get it cheaply enough to do the necessary repairs and bring it back up to snuff. A smartphone with a bad battery and cracked screen isn't completely worthless, you just need to get it cheaply enough to justify putting a new screen and new battery in it, while still leaving some profit to sell after completed.

I was happy to know this 4-bedroom house was not yet listed on the Internet or anywhere else. This was a direct advantage for me, knowing I did not have any immediate competition from other investors who would bid up the price and cause me to pay more than I wanted to pay or could pay. I could not get an asking price out of my fellow realtor buddy who was representing the seller, so I went to the 4-bedroom house on Kissimmee Street and assessed all the damages and repairs necessary.

After putting my numbers together, I decided the home was worth about $65k to me in its present condition. I went back to the office and talked with my buddy and expressed to him that $65k would be my top dollar.

To my surprise, he had already informed a few other investors like me of the potential property for sale, and there were currently multiple offers on the table.

Knowing there were other interested parties made me a little bit discouraged. I hate bidding wars, unless I'm on the selling side, of course. In the back of my mind, I could justify a slightly higher purchase price than $65k. After being bid up by a few other investors, Britney and I finally locked in the Deal at $75k. This was a fair Deal, and I knew it would be something to keep me going, as well as make my money work for me, because as Robert Kiyosaki says, "savers are losers and cash is trash."

## Ds of the Deal

I almost never have a lot of money in my bank account, because it's always invested in the next Deal and the next Deal and the next Deal. After making the necessary repairs and cosmetic updates, we ended up having about $100k invested. I had anticipated that the ARV—After Repair Value—would be between $140k and $150k. That is what I had based most of my numbers on, and that was what I had anticipated the property would appraise for when we went to refinance.

To my surprise, the appraisal on the Kissimmee house came back at a whopping $170k, leaps and bounds higher than we had budgeted for and anticipated. That the appraisal came in much higher than anticipated solidified the fact that it was okay to be bid up more than $10k in the process of purchasing this home.

**Ds of the Deal**

The main reason we got such a Deal on the Kissimmee house was because there was a Death. The children of the deceased inherited the home and were happy to unload it on us. Even though this Deal was profitable for us, it was also very profitable for the kids who sold it. They got what they wanted, cash money upfront, and sold the home AS IS, no contingencies, no inspections, no seller repairs, a very quick, easy, clean transaction. I was happy for them, and happy for myself and Britney. Seek win-win situations, especially when it comes to your business.

# D 2 - Divorce

*Divorce is one of the most financially traumatic things you can go through.*

**Richard Wagner**

I knew a man who lost everything in a Divorce, including his wife, his business, his assets. This really took a hit on his productivity. He started liquidating everything he owned, real estate and other assets, including his boat. He lived close to a lake and owned a luxurious boat with all the bells and whistles. This boat was worth about $30k at the time. He basically gave it away for only $15k because he didn't want to hassle with anything anymore. While the boat sold for less than it was worth, it provided a quick solution for this Divorced gentleman to unload another potential headache.

As a real estate broker, much of my income is made through generating commissions selling real estate. I love buying and selling, and have since I

## Ds of the Deal

was young. One of my many current occupations is helping buyers and sellers of real estate. I specialize in helping families purchase the home that is right for them, and helping people sell their home as they transition in life.

There are many reasons why a buyer or a seller would buy a property or sell a property, and regardless of the reason, I am the solution. I started out as a real estate agent—a realtor. After two years, I became a real estate broker, the highest office in real estate sales. I love my job, I love people, and I love solving problems.

Most people who are buying a property or selling property are usually one of a few things, including stressed out, detail oriented, excited, happy, nervous. It is a blast handling all those emotions and helping buyers and sellers. I absolutely love what I do, but only to a certain point. Too much of anything can stress a person out, right?

For this Divorce chapter, we will go over a Deal where I represented a first-time home buyer couple, Nile and Brittany. I had nurtured them for almost two years. By nurturing, I mean constantly answering real estate questions, running comparables for them, and sharing potential first homes with them. When they were finally in a position to buy, I got them prequalified with a local lender who does a good job.

After getting them prequalified, we got our list of homes together and jumped in the truck to go see them. After looking at half a dozen or more homes, this first-time homebuyer couple chose the one that worked best for them. I called the listing realtor in hopes of getting the scoop on this home. As we chatted, I put the pieces together. The seller was going through a Divorce, and desperately wanted simply to be done with the house.

Although this may be a more vulnerable position for the seller, it was a great time to be a buyer, or the buyer's realtor. I relayed this information to my clients, Nile and Brittany. We decided to not only send a lowball offer, but request that the seller pay the closing costs and

# Ds of the Deal

buyer's lender fees. This would save my clients many thousands of dollars.

For you to understand the situation better, the Missouri real estate market at that time was extremely hot. Homes were selling for as much as $20k over listing price, creating an extreme home shortage. Homes were selling within seconds, not weeks. You were lucky to get a house for full price, and could almost anticipate having to pay thousands over list price to secure the home you desired.

All things considered, we still saw fit to send an offer that was almost $20k below what the home was worth. The offer was received. Lo and behold, we were able to work the Deal out at an undeniably low purchase price for my buyers.

After the offer had been accepted, we went about the normal home buying process. We went through the inspection period and got every single repair recommended by the home inspector, either paid for or repaired by the seller. The buyer's lender got an appraisal on the property before issuing the loan. Said appraisal came in thousands of dollars higher than the purchase price, giving my buyers even more instant equity.

Why would a seller accept such a low offer, especially in such a hot market? What went

## Ds of the Deal

through the seller's head, we may not know, but what we do know is that we were the best solution to her problem at that moment. Although the seller might have gotten more money by holding out, we were the best offer at that particular time on that particular day. The seller consented and accepted our offer, creating a win-win situation. A win for the seller because she was able to liquidate an asset while going through Divorce. A win for the buyers because they immediately had a piggy bank of equity on purchasing the home.

Of course, it was a win for me, because as the buyer's realtor, I received a commission from the seller for bringing a buyer.

## Ds of the Deal

All things aside, do your best to be the solution to someone's problem. Do you know someone who is going through a Divorce? Make them an offer they can't refuse on assets they are trying to liquidate. You may be surprised at how a win-win situation can benefit everyone involved while still giving you the good Deal.

Who do you know who may have recently had a Divorce? Who do you know who may be going through a Divorce today?

Why not reach out to them and offer to be the solution to part of their situation, creating a win-win transaction.

**Ds of the Deal** ─────────────

# D 3 - Disease

*There are all sorts of... diseases to profit from.*

**Anne Wojcicki**

In this same hot seller's market described in the Divorce section, I was able to help a more seasoned couple get a great Deal on a home. The coronavirus pandemic, COVID-19, was spreading across the world, a virus that mainly affected older people, and relatively few younger people.

This seasoned couple was a little more detail-oriented than most, and definitely looking for a low-priced Deal. The task of finding a low-priced Deal would not be easy given the hot real estate market, in some ways due to a home shortage resulting from the coronavirus scare.

Again, homes were going for tens of thousands more than list price. How was I going to get this seasoned couple a good Deal that they and I felt comfortable about that would put them in a good equity position? I showed them dozens of nice

## Ds of the Deal

homes big enough for them and their five kids, earning every penny of the commission I soon would receive for selling them a home.

After much looking and many hours, we finally found a home that would suit their needs. The only problem was that the purchase price was not where they wanted it to be, which didn't stop me at all. In fact, it actually gave me more motivation to get them a low price. They needed a low-price Deal. We decided to make an offer on this perfect home, an offer that would more than likely offend the seller.

After making this significantly low offer, we waited. After waiting a normal amount of time, we got a phone call. To our surprise, we received confirmation from the seller that the owner would, in fact, accept our low offer. We were astounded. The Deal kept moving forward, and the closer we

## Ds of the Deal

got to closing, the more excited this big family got.

Through the grapevine of the local real estate industry, common to every local real estate market, I learned that the seller of this big house had recently lost a spouse to COVID-19. Suddenly, it made sense, the reason why we got such a low purchase price on this home: there was a Disease.

We did not know before making the offer, but this Disease/virus put the sellers in a position where they were more lenient on price. We couldn't have known, but the surviving spouse was ready to liquidate the property quickly because of the recent Disease in the family, which helped my clients get a better Deal.

Disease and deteriorating health are no joking matter. Many people suffer daily, and those people need solutions to their daily struggles. My buyers were one solution for the surviving spouse. We were able to promptly help her out of a situation where she wanted and needed help.

It was a mutually beneficial transaction. The buyers got the purchase price they needed, the seller unloaded an asset she needed to unload, and both realtors made a commission for the sale.

**Ds of the Deal**

Never go soliciting hospitals to find people who are deteriorating or coping with Disease, but keep your eyes open to others and what is going on in their lives.

You may be able to be the best solution to one of their problems at the moment.

How can you help someone who is currently suffering from Disease? Is there anyone in that situation who could benefit from your services? How can you create a win-win situation with someone who is Disease ridden?

# Ds of the Deal

# D 4 - Desperate

*When you are desperate, it's usually because of fear.*

**Marelisa Fábrega**

There will be times in the global market—or your local market—where people get spooked and feel they *need* to sell. Whether selling vehicles or other assets or liabilities, shifts in the market often seem to spook people and make them want to sell.

This shake up in the market has happened many, many times in the past.

Take a look at the Great Depression in the 1930s that followed the Roaring 20s when everyone made money hand over fist. No doubt there were Desperate people in the Great Depression looking to unload assets for cash just to put food on their table.

## Ds of the Deal

Another example of a market shift was 2008 when the U.S. housing market collapsed. Some cities and states got hit harder than others, but overall, people panicked and were Desperate to the point of *needing* to sell assets just to get by.

Desperate is an interesting and important D of the Deal. Let me tell you what was happening in the year 2020.

For much of the year there was a coronavirus pandemic. Whether the virus was man-made or as lethal as many made it out to be, people panicked. There was a lot of panic worldwide, including in the United States. This panic, this Desperation, caused people to sell and liquidate assets.

Whether selling to get out of stocks, homes, rental properties, or primary residences, many people were spooked and feeling some of the Desperation that was felt in the Great Depression and housing market crash of 2008.

I was aware of this opportunity to solve someone's problem by making a lower offer on their assets.

Their problem of *needing* to sell and put cash in their pocket would be solved. My problem of *needing* to grow my investment portfolio would be solved.

## Ds of the Deal

I noticed a growing influx of people listing their houses FSBO, For Sale By Owner. More specifically, I saw people suddenly listing their houses FSBO on Facebook.

Facebook Marketplace is a beauty, and I don't know how we lived without it.

One of my morning rituals during the COVID-19 pandemic was to scroll through Facebook Marketplace and see what Deals were there. I was open to a Deal on anything, a motorcycle, a car, or a tool, but was more specifically looking for real estate I could acquire and profit from, adding to Britney's and my rental portfolio.

In the midst of this COVID-19 pandemic and halfway through the year 2020, I jumped on Facebook Marketplace in the morning, as usual. I saw a 4-bedroom, 2-bathroom, 2-car garage, 2000-square-foot home listed FSBO.

What appealed to me about this house was the great location, potential equity, and of course, the list price.

It turned out the little old lady who posted her property FSBO on Facebook listed it for the same price she paid for it years prior.

**Ds of the Deal**

This meant the house was deeply underpriced compared to the 2020 market. I immediately messaged this little old lady, inquiring about the house and asking to set up a showing.

# Ds of the Deal

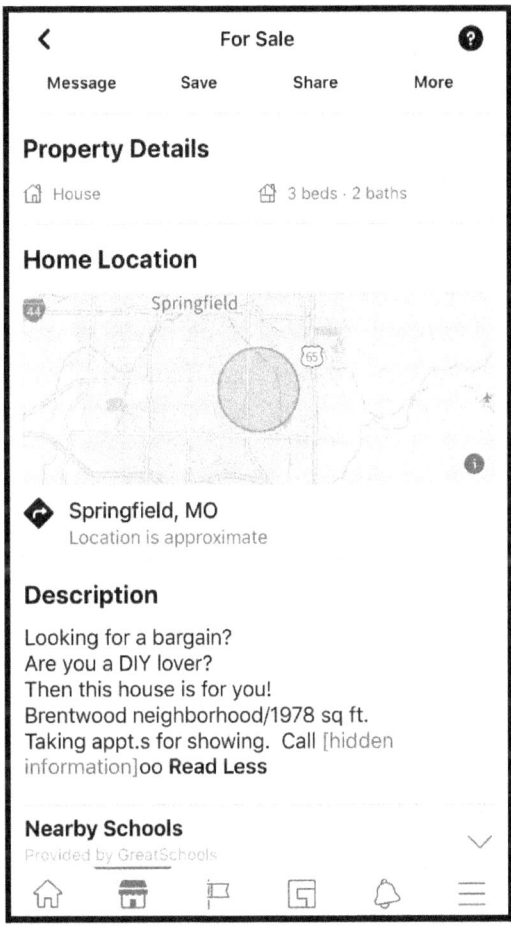

I wanted to see the inside of the property in person and not just base my offer on pictures in the ad. Talking with her, I found out a dozen or more other people had messaged her, all probably thinking the same thing I was: the home was underpriced and had potential for a Deal. She told

## Ds of the Deal

me she already had showings lined up back-to-back later in the day. I wanted to get a showing before everyone else because I was able to make a cash offer.

The others looking at the property had a standard bank loan offer with contingencies, appraisal, and inspections. I quickly established the fact that my offer would be cash, as is, no contingencies, no inspections, close quickly, with no fees or commissions.

After I lined out these terms, she agreed to meet me at the house before her other showings later in the day. I found out this was, in fact, an old rental house, which was music to my ears. I can't count the number of retiring landlords I've talked to who are fed up with rental properties. Many long-time landlords are just burnt out, because it is easy to get burnt out with rental properties. It was no wonder this little old grandma was fed up with her previous renters, who had stiffed her on the last two rent payments, left the house trashed, and refused to leave. She had to get a court order with a police officer to remove them from the property.

Situations like that, where the owner/seller is stressed out and fed up, provide a great opportunity for a Deal. Walking through the home, I knew this property was a steal. It was in

# Ds of the Deal

an up-and-coming area of town, right next to the mall and many big businesses, as well as many other homes that were more expensive than this one. Imagine a dollhouse neighborhood made up of super cute, clean-cut 3- and 4-bedroom homes. That is what this neighborhood looked like.

You'll see as you buy/sell or do anything related to real estate that location is key, location, location, location. You can change everything about a property except its location. All it takes is money, but the one thing that can't be fixed is location. Long story short, the location was amazing and the $100k price was low. Me being a Hustler by nature, I naturally tried to beat this little old lady down on price. I offered $5k less than list price, and she said no. I offered $3k less and she said no. I offered $2,500 less than list price and she said no. In one last attempt to get at least some discount, I offered $99k, only $1k less than her list price.

At that point, I thought we were so close on price that she would take my offer right away and we could move on to closing. But do you know what she said? "I will think about it." I couldn't believe this little lady was about to blow the Deal over $1k. I knew a dozen other people were lined up to purchase this home, as I saw the messages other potential buyers were sending her. I left my written offer of $99k with her.

She reviewed it with her attorney and called me back the next day and accepted my offer. We met at the title company and both signed the offer which we gave to the title company to process.

We used Meridian Title Company, people I trust, who have done a lot of Deals for me. The seller wanted to use a title company that was a little cheaper, but my title company price-matched, so we got it done at my title company.

Less than two weeks later, we closed on the property and the lady was as pleased as can be. Later, she mentioned that my cash offer had seemed "a little too good to be true," and she had been antsy as to whether we would actually close or not.

As I had promised at the time of the offer, we did close on time. I proceeded to remodel the property and make it brand new again, creating some great equity in the home as well as adding a great rental to our portfolio. Again, it was a complete win-win situation, and it was all because this little old lady was Desperate and I provided a solution to her Desperation.

## Ds of the Deal

Who do you know that may be Desperate? How can you be the solution to the problem? What would be mutually beneficial for you and the person in Desperation?

# D 5 - Debt

*If you're trying to get out of debt, you have to be willing to treat everything as expendable.*

**Phil McGraw**

Debt is an interesting thing. Almost everyone has debt. Our country, the United States of America, is far into the hole of Debt. Much of the money in circulation in the world is Debt. Debt can work for you or against you. In 2003, the savings of Americans went in the negative, meaning that people were spending more than they were making. With credit cards, home loans, car loans, personal loans, business loans, government grants, opportunity zone funds, there are an almost indefinite number of ways to get into Debt.

Stores and product producers run more ads and enticements to buy than ever. With YouTube ads, Instagram ads, Google ads, TV ads, newspaper ads, and many more types of

## Ds of the Deal

advertisements, it almost looks like we are under attack. There are so many ads and enticements it is no wonder that Americans tend to spend more than they make.

Debt is bad for people who do not have self-control or who spend too much. Debt is good for people who have self-control and know how to use debt to their advantage. Debt can be a tool for creating and growing wealth. For example, Britney and I have much Debt, millions of dollars. But all our debt is more than canceled out by monthly payments from our renters.

There is a difference between good Debt, business or industrial Debt, and consumer Debt, credit cards for entertainment or clothes or eating out Debt. Consumer Debt is scary, because the only one paying it off is you. Business Debt is different because you usually have employees or tenants or others who help you manage and pay off that Debt.

It is usually people who have much consumer Debt who file bankruptcy and lose their assets and go to foreclosure. It is almost as frequently the people with business Debt or business savvy who swoop in and pick up the pieces and get good Deals on assets that the consumer Debt people are losing.

# Ds of the Deal

What category do you fit in? Do you have business Debt or consumer Debt? Do you know the difference?

I vividly remember the first Debt I ever had. The reason I created this Debt would make sense to any 16-year-old out there. There was an extremely clean, very tight, luxurious BMW convertible that I had my eye on. It was a 1996 BMW 328CI Blue Convertible 5-Speed Manual V6 Sports Car. What was so intriguing about this car was not just the heated seats and clean title, but more so the low mileage on the vehicle, a mere 88k miles. For a car that was a few decades old, 88k miles wasn't much.

The owner of this luxurious BMW was my future father-in-law, the dad of my girlfriend, Britney. Britney and I are married now, but this BMW lust took place while we were still in high school, both 16 years old. As a 16-year-old, I had already sold a few vehicles, including motorcycles and cars. I was familiar with buying and selling because I was born to do it. It sometimes feels like I came out of the womb selling. Buying and selling is one of my God-given talents.

I saw this extremely nice BMW that my girlfriend's dad owned. Britney's dad had to teach me how to drive a stick, driving all around town, including and especially uphill. Every time I

## Ds of the Deal

jumped into the BMW with Britney's dad, I was more and more sold on it, even though it wasn't for sale. I floated the idea to Britney's dad that I was interested in the car and might buy it from him. He threw out a price of $3k that seemed reasonable and fair.

The only problem was I didn't have $3k. Through all my buying and selling and trading until that point I had saved $2k cash, short of what I needed to buy this awesome BMW. I asked some friends and family, trying to borrow $1k to

## Ds of the Deal

make this Deal work, but I had no luck. I told Britney's dad of my predicament, that I only had $2k of the $3k he wanted. He, being a PhD professor/university department head, decided this was the perfect opportunity to teach me a life lesson. He said he would finance the other $1k, essentially creating a monthly car payment for me. In the name of principle, he charged me interest.

If I remember correctly, the interest rate was low, about 2% APR. My monthly payment was a grand total of $80. This was the first time I'd had a reoccurring monthly payment. As silly as it sounds, I was a little stressed out. I wanted the car, though, so I agreed to his terms and we signed some sort of "promise to pay" note. I rounded up a few buddies to show them the awesome car I was whipping around town. I also included the fact that I now had a monthly car payment. For a bunch of 16-year-old boys who had never had car payments, we were in awe. One of my buddies, Sterling, who had built up a good savings account, confided in me that he would loan me money if I couldn't make my monthly payment in the future.

Looking back, $80 a month seems minuscule compared to the tens of thousands of dollars my wife and I owe the banks each month on our

## Ds of the Deal

rental properties. It was a place to start, though, and it was a great life lesson, especially the part about having to pay interest to my future father-in-law.

What was your first monthly payment? What was your first Debt?

The reason for this introduction into Debt is because many good Deals can come from Debt. Debt on a house that remains unpaid pushes that house into foreclosure. Buying a foreclosure as an investor intending to fix it up and profit by either flipping or renting is a great Deal.

I have personal experience with Debt leading straight to a good Deal. There was a nice 3-bedroom, 1-bathroom, 1-car garage house in a B+ neighborhood. The homeowner, for whatever reason, stopped making the mortgage payments. The bank, of course, repossessed the property and foreclosed on it, then put the house on the real estate market to sell and hopefully recoup some if not all of the money owed.

This foreclosure was a great opportunity to not only get a commission check, but to help out one of my investor clients by getting a great Deal. It was only a great Deal because it was in foreclosure and the bank was willing to take a fairly low offer. Foreclosures are often a Deal

**Ds of the Deal**

because of the Debt the bank is trying to recuperate.

As soon as I saw this foreclosure hit the market, I floated it out to my investor and got him in the door of this home so we could assess the amount needed for repairs. We assessed the repair cost, and made an offer on the property.

Our offer was almost 30 percent less than the list price. Happily, our offer was accepted and we closed on the property two weeks later. Like the phrase we all know and love, "the early bird gets the worm", that's how this Deal was.

We were the first to know about the foreclosure, the first people in the door, the first people to make an offer.

## Ds of the Deal

The reason this home was even for sale was because of the Debt/foreclosure situation. The reason why our low offer was accepted was because the bank was trying to recoup some of the Debt they had on the property. Debt can provide good Deals.

Again, most people are overwhelmed with Debt, Debt on their cars, Debt on credit cards, Debt on houses, which is all fine and dandy until they stop paying. When people stop paying down the Debt they get in a crunch, and that provides an opportunity for you to get a Deal.

With this little foreclosure house I sold to one of my investors, everyone was a winner. The previous owner was a winner because he did not have to Deal with the property anymore, the bank was a winner because they recouped as much Debt as they could, I was a winner because I gained a commission from selling this property, and—most importantly—my client was a winner because he got a great Deal.

Fast forward three months after the closing/purchase of this foreclosure home. My investor client made the property brand new, updated and remodeled with no remaining issues. The property appraised so high that my client doubled his money. In just three months, my client doubled his money because he bought a house that was in the middle of the Debt/foreclosure process. Debt is a killer for those who don't know how to manage it, but Debt is also crucial and a step up for those who know how to use it.

How can you use Debt to further your business? What kind of Debt do you currently have? Can you differentiate what is consumer Debt and what is business Debt in your life? How can you eliminate or lessen your consumer Debt?

# D 6 - Dated

*New things are always better than old things.*

**Andy Warhol**

Picture a Dated property. What would a Dated property entail? For me, the first thing I think when I hear *Dated* is wallpaper, lots and lots of wallpaper. You know the type of wallpaper I'm talking about, the floral kind, usually a few layers thick, with wallpaper bordering where the walls and ceilings meet. The second thing I think when I hear *Dated* is pink and green tile. Have you seen a bathroom that was built in the 1960s or 1970s? More often than not, there is vibrant pink or green tile lining the walls and/or bathtub surround.

What else do you think of? Out of style? I think of wood paneling. Many homes built in the 1900s have lots and lots of wood paneling. I'm sure you've seen it, and you know it is not effective at retaining heat or air. Wood paneling was a staple that many older homes still have. Some people

## Ds of the Deal

paint over paneling, and others rip it out and replace with drywall.

What other characteristics come with a Dated home? With window technology getting better and better, old wooden windows are definitely Dated.

In almost every remodel, new windows replace outdated windows. New vinyl, double-pane energy-efficient windows are much more appealing than old, wood single-pane windows that let heat and cool escape or enter the home easily.

In the modern real estate market, most people define the woodgrain color as dated. You know what woodgrain color is, it's just the color of normal wood.

The hip thing to do these days is to have white trim and gray walls. If you have wood trim that looks like wood, it may be classified as Dated.

Taking all of these things into account—the wallpaper, the pink and green tile, the woodgrain trim, the wood paneling—if you found a home that had every one of these features, would you pay top dollar for it? No, of course not. Why pay top dollar for something that is not in top-dollar shape?

## Ds of the Deal

Finding something that is Dated can provide an opportunity for a Deal, often a fixer-upper. In every city across the world, there are homes that are more updated than others. It's harder to get a Deal on a home that's already been remodeled and flipped.

It is much easier to get a Deal on a property that has yet to be touched and still looks like it's right out of the era of Elvis Presley or the Beatles, shag carpet at all.

Britney and I have personal experience with a Dated property, the second house we lived in. This home was extremely Dated. All the wallpaper issues and pink tile and wood paneling horrors were present in this home.

This 3-bedroom, 1.5-bath, 4-car garage home looked like it was straight out of the 70s, only lacking a vacuum tube radio or black and white television set.

Before submitting an offer to purchase this property, Britney and I took into account that it desperately needed updating. However, because of all of the needed updates, we were able to get a Deal. Sellers who have Dated products usually understand what they have is not worth top dollar.

## Ds of the Deal

This particular home my wife and I were interested in purchasing needed everything. It needed pink tile removal, old carpet removal, paneling ripped out from the kitchen, an old fireplace with a brick facade removed, old windows to be replaced with new, and worst of all, there was much wallpaper to remove. If you've ever removed wallpaper, you know what I'm talking about. Sometimes it comes off like butter, but most times it sticks like a tick to a dog.

**Ds of the Deal**

This particular seller knew the property was Dated, yet she wanted top dollar. This property had potential but was listed at a high price, probably double what it should've been. We submitted our low offer as soon as the home hit the market, and we received a hearty rejection.

We watched this home sit on the market, price reduction after price reduction. I knew that if we played the waiting game, waited until the seller got a little more reasonable, a little more Desperate, that we might get a Deal on this Dated home.

After a few months, we resubmitted the same low offer we had submitted months before. Not completely to our surprise, the seller was at the point where she understood the property was in need of some love, and that it would not bring top dollar without being in top condition.

# Ds of the Deal

Since our offer was ridiculously low, the seller countered, then we countered back, and were able to reach a Deal. We purchased the home, and started the updates immediately.

Since we were doing all of these updates out of our own pocket, our own cash reserve, the process was a little more slow going than my wife would've liked, but it was getting Done. Many months and tens of thousands of dollars later, Britney and I had a beautiful spic-and-span brand new, updated home.

Let me paint a picture for you of the updated condition of the home. This home now features beautiful, refinished, dark brown hardwood floors, heavy duty tile in the kitchen, vinyl plank gray flooring in the bathrooms, the gray walls and white trim everyone is after, vinyl double pane energy efficient windows, new drywall in the kitchen where wood paneling used to be, new drywall texture on the ceiling throughout the home.

There is a new electrical box, coupled with new outlets and switches and electric fixtures throughout the house, white painted kitchen and bathroom cabinets, as opposed to wood grain.

The little half bathroom became a full bathroom with a tub and shower.

## Ds of the Deal

There is a brand new privacy fence with double gates, able to fit a car, truck, or trailer, on each side of the home.

**Ds of the Deal**

To put it simply, this home is no longer Dated, but is extremely updated. Although it took multiple months, patience, sweat equity, and hard work, Britney and I were able to get a low-priced Deal on a Dated property, fix it up, and enjoy it. This isn't rocket science. This is something many people do all over the country and, for that matter, all over the world. Buy something that needs work, a fixer-upper, something Dated. Get

# Ds of the Deal

a cheap enough Deal on it where updating is justifiable. Then, at the end, enjoy it or turn a profit.

At the end of our Dated remodel, we decided to stay and enjoy it. We got it appraised, showing that we had gained tens of thousands of dollars in equity after subtracting our remodel expense.

This is only possible because we bought it right, meaning low-priced. Most principles in this book are based around this fact: you make your money when you buy.

All these Ds of the Deal are about buying your asset right, or buying cheap enough from the get-go. Like many of the principles discussed, Dated does not just apply to real estate. It can apply to a rusty old car that at one time had value but has become Dated.

People find distressed classic cars then fix them up and turn a profit. There is often great worth in taking something Dated and making it new again.

What Deals in your life are Dated? How can you find a Dated Deal? Is updating something older a way you would like to make profit? Just like we update our phones and our computers and other electronics, it is important to find the worth in updating assets or business opportunities.

## Ds of the Deal

An updated house is worth a lot more than a Dated house. A restored car is worth much more than a rust bucket. Updating things that are Dated may be what catapults your temporal successes.

**Ds of the Deal** ─────────────

# D 7 - Dumb

*If a man is Dumb, someone is going to get the best of him, so why not you? If you don't, you're as Dumb as he is.*

**Arnold Rothstein**

In this chapter, we use the word Dumb not in a demeaning sense, but more in the *unbelievable* sense, like dumb luck. There are Dumb Deals out there that are almost too good to be true. Find them. Use them.

Let's switch gears for a second. All the Ds of the Deal we have talked about so far have been related to real estate. Let's talk cars. You may or may not have interest in real estate or cars, but they are great industries from which you can learn how to sell.

I owned a one-year-old Toyota Tacoma SR5 4X4 Automatic Double Cab truck. I bought this truck brand new off of the lot and drove it for a full year, putting almost 25k miles on it.

**Ds of the Deal**

I loved this truck. It has helped me haul so many materials for remodels, been as reliable as can be, and had all the fancy new features that come with a new truck.

I intentionally bought the double-cab, four-door truck so Britney and I could easily haul our lovely daughter, Brynlin, and her car seat in the back.

I also intentionally got the automatic transmission—rather than the manual transmission I really wanted—because Britney wanted to drive the truck should the need arise.

## Ds of the Deal

This was my dream truck, even down to the sandstorm color, which made me feel like I was driving in the deserts of the Middle East every time I jumped into the driver's seat.

When I bought this truck, brand-new off the lot, I heard the reoccurring phrase from friends and family: "never buy new, you lose thousands of dollars the second you drive a new car off of the lot."

I knew that Toyota cars generally hold their value pretty well, especially the Tacoma trucks. I knew I was destined to lose money buying a new truck, but I planned on keeping it for at least a decade and getting good use out of it. That was the plan, at least.

Things changed after the release of the coronavirus, COVID-19. Suddenly, factories were being closed or slowed down because of social distancing rules. People were losing their jobs, and all the other things that come when a pandemic hits.

This slowed down car manufacturing, which meant there was less supply and more demand with all of the used cars on the market. New and used cars were becoming harder to find, and car dealerships were getting more scarce.

## Ds of the Deal

I remember driving through town and seeing as many as a dozen car lots out of business. There just weren't enough cars to go around.

This caused the cycle of supply and demand, nationwide. Since there was less supply in the car market, the demand for new and used cars went up.

A friend posted on Facebook about selling his 2019 Toyota Tacoma. This friend loved Toyotas, and had been driving his Tacoma for about as long as I drove mine.

The Facebook post was a picture of his Tacoma on the back of a car hauler after he sold it.

He posted with the intention of selling a few aftermarket parts he had taken off the Tacoma before selling it, but all the Comments ended up being about how much money he made off the truck.

He sold his year-old used truck for almost exactly what he paid for it new, right off the lot.

## Ds of the Deal

This got me thinking maybe it was time for me to take advantage of this COVID-19 market. I looked at other Toyota Tacoma posts on Facebook and read other reviews online.

## Ds of the Deal

After seeing about half a dozen posts and reviews, I concluded Toyota Tacomas were in extreme demand because the factories that made them had shut down. My jaw dropped time and time again as I saw used Tacomas selling for close to what they cost new. It was Dumb how much these used Toyota trucks were selling for.

It seemed the main buyer was a website called *Carvana.com*, an online company that would make you an offer within just a few minutes after you put your car information online. This company would then come to your door, load your vehicle onto the trailer, then haul it away, leaving you with a cashier's check. I realized this opportunity of selling my truck for almost even money may never come again. While I didn't agree with "you lose thousands of dollars as soon as you drive a new car off the lot," I knew my year-old, 25k-mile Tacoma had devaluated some.

After doing my due diligence, I entered my VIN on the Carvana website. Keep in mind I paid $33k for my new truck. Minutes after inputting my truck's information, I got my all cash, no contingency offer. Can you guess what it was? It was Dumb, it was insane, hardly believable. *Carvana.com* offered $32,744 for my truck. This meant I drove 25k miles in a brand new Toyota Tacoma for a full year for only $256. As you

## Ds of the Deal

know, most monthly car payments are as much as $500. I paid the equivalent of a two-week car payment in the whole year I owned and drove my truck. I was overjoyed.

That offer was better than I thought it would be. The thought of being able to get almost all my money back on my Tacoma was mind-boggling. I knew this opportunity might never come again so I accepted Carvana's offer. I set up a time for Carvana to come pick up my truck, then sat back and relaxed. A few days later, the Carvana representative with his Carvana car hauler showed up. He inspected my vehicle, verified that the title was in my name, and that everything I said was true and accurate about the truck. He started the truck, drove it onto his car hauler, and handed me a cashier's check for $32,744.

## Ds of the Deal

I felt like a king. I thought it was Dumb on Carvana's part to pay that much, but they seemed confident because there was such a high demand and low supply of used cars. They would make their money back and then some. I took that $32,744 and put it right into my bank account, which I would later use to acquire another rental property and further our rental portfolio.

Now, please don't mistake this chapter for me being thankful for COVID-19 because that's not true. What is true is that I took advantage of the market we all were in and got a ridiculous return on my Toyota Tacoma investment. I was dumbfounded for a few days after I sold my truck. I got so excited about the potential for a Deal that I plugged in the VIN numbers of all my friends and family. I plugged my wife's car in, my brother's car, my other brother's car. I even walked across the street at 10 pm to plug in my neighbor's VIN, just for fun.

About two weeks after selling my truck to *carvana.com*, I started seeing multiple posts on social media, the same Tacoma group where I had originally seen posts about Tacomas selling for extremely high prices. The posts I saw two weeks later revealed that *carvana.com* and other car buying websites and dealerships were slowing down. The same cars that were bringing $32k

## Ds of the Deal

when I sold my truck we're now bringing offers of $27k or less. The used car market was so saturated with all these cars that online and physical dealerships had bought that the demand had dropped. This made me ever so thankful for the split-second decision to sell my Tacoma when I did. If I would've hesitated on the decision to sell by even two weeks, I would have lost thousands of dollars. When you see a deal, go get it. Don't delay. There's a fine line between impulse and carpe diem. Find that fine line in your life and live on it.

After selling my Toyota Truck at the right time and for top dollar, I decided to treat myself, to go out and get my complete dream truck: a 2021 Toyota Tacoma with manual transmission, 4x4, double-cab, sunroof, wireless charging, off-road capability, and a color that no one would forget. Keep in mind, as I write this it is October 2020. I made friends at the dealership last year when I bought the brand new Toyota Tacoma. I returned to the dealership and sucked up to those guys to get myself a deal on my dream truck. After telling the what I wanted, my Toyota friends promised to keep their eyes open to find me a 2021 Toyota Tacoma months before they would be available to anybody else.

## Ds of the Deal

My friends at the dealership proved to be successful. They found my dream truck, with every feature I could imagine, down to the heated seats, sunroof, wireless charging, and coveted 6-speed manual transmission I had wished my previous Tacoma had.

As you and I have seen with my Toyota history, Toyotas hold their value. That being said, the Toyota dealership is less lenient on their sales prices because they know that Toyotas go down in value significantly more slowly than most car brands.

After going back-and-forth with my friends at the car dealership, I finally got them down to the price that I wanted, almost $4k less than the list price. I signed some papers and put down a $1k deposit on the truck. Here's the kicker: my truck

## Ds of the Deal

wasn't even built yet. I had purchased a truck so new that it had yet to be conceived.

I was able to track the manufacture process of my new Tacoma, which was being built in Texas just a few hours away. The *Ds of the Deal*, especially Done, can lead you and help you create the life you Desire. If a dream truck is what you Desire, that's what you will receive. Success is here for the taking for those who apply the *Ds of the Deal*.

There will be certain situations in your life where you will have the opportunity to get Dumb Deals, Deals that make your head spin, Deals that don't sound rational but fortunately end up panning out.

Remember, there are some unbelievable Dumb Deals to be made during pandemics or other stressful times. Like the little old lady who was concerned about coronavirus and Britney and I were able to solve her problem in the Desperate section, there are Deals to be had when everything seems to be going crazy.

We also saw this during the U.S. housing market crash in 2008. Those who had money saved in their piggy banks after the crash of 2008 were able to buy properties for pennies on the dollar, all the way until about 2016. Those were the problem solvers, the people who were prepared for and took advantage of the crash.

Entrepreneurs find ways to make money anyway, anyhow, using any means. Whether the market is up or the market is down, I don't care because I am a problem solver and I will make money by solving people's problem.

Are you currently living in a Dumb Deal time where there might be ways to profit? Of course you are. Whether you are in a recession or a booming economy, there are ways for you to find unbelievable Dumb Deals.

Have you ever been part of an unbelievably Dumb Deal? Would you like to be a part of one? What could you buy or sell that might produce a handsome profit in your current market?

# Ds of the Deal

# D 8 - Dumpy

*One man's trash is another man's treasure.*

**English Proverb**

Have you ever seen a house that was in need of some love? There are a lot of them all across the world, including where you live. The telltale cause of a Dumpy house usually is deferred maintenance or self-inflicted wear and tear by a tenant or homeowner.

Let me paint a picture of a real Dumpy house, a fixer-upper. Imagine pink shag carpet, with a cracked pink tile vanity in the bathroom. Imagine holes in the laminate floor exposing the subfloor. Think of old wooden windows, letting cold in during winter, and heat in during summer. Think of old light fixtures and burnt out electrical outlets.

Imagine an empty inground pool lined with leaves and branches on the bottom. The pool liner is caving in and there are cracks in the concrete.

## Ds of the Deal

Tree roots have busted up the concrete on the front driveway.

You open the garage and see tree roots have busted up the concrete there. Had this tree been cut down 20 years ago, the concrete would have been saved.

Think of the tens of thousands of dollars that need to be spent on this Dumpy house.

This house had potential, no doubt, but now would be classified as a Dump. This particular home in my town was listed for $130k.

## Ds of the Deal

I presented this Dumpy home to one of my investor clients who is always interested in single-family rental properties. We sat down while he ran his numbers on fixup costs to get this Dumpy home looking decent. After much thought and number crunching, he figured that the most he could pay for the home was $95k.

Right off the bat, I thought that would be quite a stretch, seeing that in our current hot real estate market homes were selling for above asking price instead of below. Reminding myself that the answer is always no if you don't ask, we put the ridiculously low $95k offer on paper.

On sending the offer to the seller's realtor, I pled my case, or I should say the case of my client. I mentioned all the Dumpy parts of the home, making it very clear that tens of thousands of dollars were necessary to bring this home up to par. There was even a question of whether the busted up driveway would cause a lawsuit if someone tripped over it and got hurt. That's how bad the driveway was.

After pleading my client's case, I put a short seven-hour deadline on our offer, which put some pressure on the seller. I made sure to keep in close contact with the seller's realtor during those seven hours. Between constant communication and justification of the Dumpy aspects of this property, we got the $95k offer accepted and signed. I was shocked, in no way expecting that offer to actually get anywhere, but we did it.

We knocked $35k off the list price, which was unheard of in that hot market, but, as always, it was a win-win situation. The seller consented and agreed to a purchase price because it was a quick cash offer. My buyer was ecstatic because he was able to acquire a new asset that would be worth fixing up and renting out since he bought it so cheap. And, of course, I made a commission on the sale. Everyone was a winner that day. Buyer, seller, buyer's realtor—me, seller's realtor, everyone. Everyone was a winner.

## Ds of the Deal

Keep your eyes open for things that are Dumpy, they just might be what you need to invest in.

What do you know that is Dumpy? What kind of Dumpy things would you like to profit on? I have a good friend who buys Dumpy riding lawnmowers and fixes them up for profit. That's his niche. Your profits don't necessarily have to come from real estate or real estate transactions. You can find Dumpy things everywhere, and make money by making those Dumpy things better.

# D 9 - Disaster

*The minute you think you've got it made, Disaster is just around the corner.*

**Joe Paterno**

In this section we are talking about Disasters, not in the sense of tornados, hurricanes, and floods, but more in the sense of a business Deal gone wrong, an unfortunate situation.

Disasters can be good or bad. It's a matter of perspective, a matter of which side of the Disaster you are on. Usually, I'm on the profiting side of the Disaster—the solution to the problem—but in this particular instance, the story I'm about to share with you, I was on the unfortunate side of Disaster.

I was representing the sellers, a great young couple who lived a faith-based, law-abiding life. This couple had two young boys, a newborn, and a toddler just figuring out life by walking and getting his hands into everything.

## Ds of the Deal

I met the father, Jared, on Craigslist. I bought a few mattress box springs from him and we struck a conversation. I just started asking questions and being social. I quickly found out that he worked for a local lumber/hardware store and that he was quite handy when it came to window and door installation.

That was music to my ears. Britney and I are always putting new windows into our new rental houses, and we had a few that needed sliding glass doors. I asked what he would charge for a window or door installation, and he was reasonable, so I gave him some work.

About a year after our first contact, Jared reached out to me to get their home SOLD. I quickly ran all my comparable numbers. After assessing the home value, we listed the house for sale.

This house was a spacious 3-bedroom, 1-bathroom house with a kitchen area, dining area, and living area.

There was also an unfinished basement that provided a 1-car garage and plenty of storage space.

**Ds of the Deal**

We listed this home for $119k. With the real estate market being so on fire due to the shortage of homes on the market, we got multiple offers the first day. These offers bid each other up to $128,300. My sellers were ecstatic because they were getting almost $10k more than the list price. The buyers were happy that they were securing the home they wanted in such a hot real estate market. It looked like we would have smooth sailing and that everything would work out great.

Well, everything did not work out great. When it came time to appraise this home, as the buyer's lender required and as most lenders do, the knot head appraiser appraised the house at only $113k, or $15k less than what buyer and seller had agreed to.

## Ds of the Deal

My sellers were down, feeling sick to their stomachs with frustration. This meant the home could not sell for the original contract price of $128,300. If the sellers proceeded with the sale they would lose almost $15k. If that's not a Disaster, I don't know what is. I begged and pleaded with the appraiser.

I sent comparables over to justify the original higher purchase price. I did everything in my power to sway the appraiser's opinion of value, without result. The hardheaded appraiser wouldn't budge or adjust her appraisal report from her original low appraisal.

Unfortunately, my sellers were in a pinch, already under contract to purchase a new home. They needed the proceeds of the sale of their home to make their new home purchase work. My sellers took it in the shorts and sold the house at the lesser appraised value of only $113k.

It was a Disaster because the buyer's lending bank would not make a loan at the original agreed purchase price of $128,300.

The bank would only allow a purchase price of what the appraisal value showed.

**Ds of the Deal**

My sellers were so frustrated and discouraged, but this was the only way to get them into their new house and keep their Deal going. The buyer was the real winner that day, getting a house way cheaper than the agreed to price. So the moral of this story is the buyer got a great Deal. We had a Disaster with that appraisal, and the buyer profited, while the sellers had to take the loss.

## Ds of the Deal

In the long run, though, it was still a win-win for the sellers because they were able to move up and purchase a bigger and better home. They just didn't have as much cash left over as they had hoped.

Have you experienced a Disaster? What side were you on during your Disaster? Did you profit or did you lose?

# D 10 - Dropped Out of Contract

*Fall Through: To fail or stop in a sudden or final way.*

**Merriam-Webster Dictionary**

The term Dropped Out of Contract frequently is used when a Deal falls through in real estate. You could Drop Out of Contract for a variety of reasons. For example, that young couple we talked about in the Disaster section could have Dropped Out of Contract on receiving the low $113k appraisal, but they decided to stick it out and take the loss.

Appraisals can kill Deals and cause things to Drop Out of Contract.

Home inspections can also cause Deals to Drop Out of Contract, which I've seen many times. The typical situation is that the buyer gets an inspection on a home that reveals problems they had not imagined would be wrong.

## Ds of the Deal

Cold feet can also cause a house to Drop Out of Contract. Sometimes sellers decide they no longer want to sell, or buyers no longer want or no longer need to buy, causing a Drop Out of Contract situation.

A buyer not being able to secure financing can cause a Drop Out of Contract.

In my experience, you are more likely to get a better Deal as a home buyer if the home has Dropped Out of Contract. A Dropped Out of Contract home most likely has an already completed inspection report, which saves the new buyer $400-$500. The seller may have already done a handful of repairs from said inspection report. Often, the seller may be more eager to liquidate the property having had a bad experience.

Here's a personal experience. I represented a family moving from Arizona to Missouri. Fortunately, we were all on the same page on the type of home they needed and their price range. They were already prequalified with a local lender. Everything was looking good except that we were unable to secure a place in Missouri because homes were selling so quickly and for top dollar. What was most important to this family was acreage. They were eager to become landowners

## Ds of the Deal

and welcomed everything that came with owning land.

We spent quite some time looking at houses, FaceTiming with them at every potential property because they were still in Arizona. Finally, we found the right property, a spacious 4-bedroom, 3-bathroom, 3,300-square-foot home on 15 acres. Included were multiple shop buildings and a completely self-sufficient 1-bedroom, 1-bathroom, 2-car garage apartment building. This property was perfect for their needs.

The reason we hadn't found this property earlier was because it had been under contract the whole time. When I saw this home as Dropped Out of Contract, I called the listing agent to get the lowdown on the property and why it had Dropped Out of Contract. As often happens, the previous buyers were unable to secure financing,

## Ds of the Deal

which left the sellers in that awkward position created when a property Drops Out of Contract. The sellers thought their home was sold, until it wasn't. The sellers were banking on the fact that the previous buyers were going to get a loan, which they didn't.

That provided a great opportunity for me and my Arizona buyers. It was an opportunity for us to save the day. The sellers lowered the price by $10k, hoping to get the house sold right away. We became the solution the sellers needed, and the buyers got a great Deal.

We made an offer that was a little less than the reduced asking price and got the Deal. The sellers were happy with our terms and my Arizona buyers were ecstatic. This property was everything they wanted, and a total bang for the buck.

To our surprise, the best was yet to come. We thought nothing out of the ordinary when it came time for the buyer's lender to get an appraisal on the property.

As mentioned, unless the appraiser is having a really bad day or is being extra picky, the appraiser usually establishes an appraised value right at or slightly more than the purchase price stated on the contract. For example, if a buyer is

# Ds of the Deal

buying a house for $100k, the appraiser will look at the accepted $100k offer and appraise the house for $101k. It's rare that an appraiser would go much higher than the contract price, maybe because they feel it's unnecessary.

The appraisal for this gorgeous home on 15 acres came in $12k more than the purchase price. The most I had seen up until that point was about $7k appraised value beyond the purchase price.

In my opinion, this high appraisal of the home meant the property was actually worth at least $20k more than the purchase price, as it is so rare that an appraiser would be so high above purchase price to begin with.

What the appraiser should do, of course, is actually estimate the true value of a property. It shouldn't matter what the purchase price is, but it seems the purchase price on the contract often sways the final appraisal amount. But like everything, there is variety. We sure wished the couple in the Disaster section had an appraiser who appraised their home at the purchase price.

Long story short, this beautiful home on 15 acres with a private apartment building and many shops were sold at a great price to my buyers because of the previous Drop Out of Contract.

## Ds of the Deal

Dropping Out of Contract isn't something that just relates to real estate, though.

A Deal falling through or flaking out is virtually the same thing as Dropping Out of Contract, and can relate to a car sale that has a buyer back out, or any private-party item for sale on Facebook Marketplace that has had a buyer flake out.

Keep your eye open for Deals that have Dropped Out of Contract, or in other words, have had a buyer flake out.

Do you believe you can get a good Deal on something that Dropped Out of Contract? I encourage you to find those Dropped Out of Contract situations and get the Deal.

# D 11 - Done

*The best way to guarantee a loss is to quit.*

**Morgan Freeman**

Have you ever known someone to be fed up? Done? Maybe frustrated or ready to move on? Finding someone who is Done has potential for a Deal. Let me show you why.

My wife and I bought a new-construction home. Before that, we lived in a quaint 3-bedroom, 2-bathroom, 4-car garage, 1,200-square-foot cookie-cutter home. This home—featured in *Hustle Then Repeat*—had been a great asset for us. I could have lived there forever, mostly because it was paid off with no home loan or mortgage, just a HELOC. I knew, though, that with our growing family we would need a bigger home with more bedrooms and bathrooms, more square footage.

After having lived in our quaint little 3-bedroom home for almost two years, Britney and I started

## Ds of the Deal

looking—just to see—what nicer homes were out there. Britney had promised we would spend at least five years in our little home before making a switch. As we were only two years into that five-year plan, I thought I was safe in just looking around at other homes. In hindsight, I should have known that because we were looking, we were getting more and more into the mood to buy every day.

We eventually got to the point of writing an offer on a very nice new 4-bedroom, 2-bathroom, 3-car garage home. Our offer was too low, and we moved on. After months of looking around, one particular new construction caught my eye. It was a glorious 4k-square-foot, 5-bedroom, 3-bathroom, 3-car garage home. This home caught my eye because the list price per square foot was so much less than virtually every other new construction home on the market in our region.

At the time, it was typical to see a new home listed for $140 per square foot, meaning that a 1k-square-foot new construction home would list for about $140k. I was used to seeing $100 per square foot on remodeled homes that had just been fixed up, and had even seen a few very basic new construction homes for sale at $125 per square foot.

## Ds of the Deal

Just out of curiosity, take a look at new homes being built in your area right now. How much are those homes costing per square foot?

This particular 5-bedroom, 3-bathroom, 3-car garage, almost 4k-square-foot home was listed for only $89 per square foot. I couldn't believe a new construction of this caliber, in this area of town, could be listed even remotely that cheap. I looked at the DOM, Days on Market, and saw it had been listed earlier that day. I might have been one of the first people to even see it listed. I sent the link to my wife for her to review. We hustled out to the house as soon as we could to get a glimpse of the construction site. This was an unusual direction for us, buying a big house and getting into a big monthly payment. I had made about $25k in real estate commissions the previous month, so I was feeling pretty good about our finances and felt like we could afford the high payment.

After walking through that home, Britney and I were sold. It felt like home to us. More importantly, it wouldn't cost us an arm and a leg to have this luxurious home. Still, I was a little apprehensive, and questioning the low price. I had seen many 20-year-old homes sell for much more per square foot. I called the builder's realtor. After talking, it was apparent that the

## Ds of the Deal

builder had a new project at a different location on his mind, and was Done with building this home. He was Done. Finished. Not Done in the literal sense, because there was still carpet and fixtures and exterior siding work that needed doing, but Done in a figurative sense. His heart was out of the project, no more, nada, zip. He was Done.

I found out that unless we came in close to full list price, the seller/builder would have to bring money to the closing table just to get the Deal done. It seemed as though he was okay with breaking even on this house because he had bigger and better things in his future. I was overjoyed.

With some couples, the husband and wife have different roles and expectations in the homebuying process. The wife often looks for an aesthetically pleasing home, a cute master bathroom and spacious kitchen. The husband often thinks about the monthly payment, "what's this gonna cost me?" That's exactly how Britney and I were. We loved this house because it was super cute, super new, with granite countertops, vinyl plank flooring, an appealing exterior, with a bathtub and separate shower in the master, as well as spacious living areas. I, on the other hand, could not get past the fact that it was only $89 per square foot. Of course, there were a few other things I loved, the three-car garage, second-story wooden back deck where I could go through my business calls and relax.

All in all, this house was perfect for us, and we knew it. We scrambled to get our finances in order, and sent a lowball offer of almost $20k less than asking price to the builder. The builder, of course, rejected that and countered back with almost full price. We went ahead and accepted this counter offer, because we knew that even though we are paying almost full price, this home was an absolute bargain, something we could turn around and sell for a profit just a few short months later, if desired.

On getting prequalified for the loan, and accepting the builder's counter offer, we were officially under contract to purchase the home. I was ecstatic, my wife was overjoyed, and the builder was glad to move on to his next big project. He was glad to be Done with this house that he was now building for my wife and me.

Or so we thought....

**Ds of the Deal** ─────────────

# D 12 - Decline

*If someone offered me a free trip to the International Space Station, I would decline. I like Earth. I like the Internet. I like Diet Coke. I have cats. I write about brave people. I'm not one of them.*

**Andy Weir**

Britney and I loved everything about this new house because of its many outstanding features and because it was only $89 per square foot. There was no question that this house was perfect for us, and we knew it.

After getting prequalified for the loan, and accepting the builder's counter offer, we were officially under contract to purchase the home. Our prequalification from the bank was contingent on my father-in-law, Britney's father, cosigning on the loan with us. A cosigner on a loan just means that if you fail to make the monthly payment, your cosigner agrees to make the payment for you. Britney and I could have afforded the home on our own, with no cosigner needed, had we not taken so many tax write-offs and had so many business expenses in the previous calendar year. As you will see when you buy property and deal with banks, they all want to see high income on previous tax returns.

The standard amount a bank needs to see before issuing a loan is two years of previous tax returns. Since our last two tax return numbers were low, Britney's dad agreed to cosign so we could get the loan for this awesome new construction home. I was ecstatic, my wife was overjoyed, and the builder was glad he was able to move on to his next project and be rid of this house.

Our closing date was set about 60 days from the time we accepted the builder's counter offer. About 45 days into that 60-day period, this deal took a turn. After much thought and analyzation, Britney and I realized that this home, as glorious and as cheap as it was, might be what pushed us over the edge toward bankruptcy.

Our home, the little 3-bedroom, 2-bathroom, 4-car garage home, was paid off and we had no mortgage. This new home would create a monthly mortgage of almost $2k.

## Ds of the Deal

Britney and I realized that as successful as we were becoming, we were still in our growing phase. Our goal was to acquire mortgages that other people pay, not mortgages that we would have to pay. The way you acquire a mortgage that someone else pays off for you is by acquiring an investment property and placing a tenant who pays you rent, which allows you to pay the mortgage with no money out of pocket.

Britney and I scrutinized this new construction house deal day and night. We loved the house. We so desperately wanted the house, and it was being offered at a great price.

Unfortunately, though, we had to admit it just wasn't in line with our financial goals, or what we could easily afford at the time. Britney's Dad was no longer available to cosign on the loan, so we reluctantly decided to terminate the deal, to Decline the purchase of that home.

It wasn't easy being in that situation, having to Decline an awesome new home. Many people were mad at me. The builder and the builder's realtor were extremely upset, of course. Britney even said a few choice words after I told her we were no longer able to get the home.

To Decline a home that nice made me feel sick. I felt badly for Britney, a little bummed for myself,

# Ds of the Deal

but I felt even worse for the builder who had taken the home off the market for 45 days in preparation of the sale to us.

Britney and I had put $1k of earnest money down at the time we wrote the offer. Earnest money is money paid to confirm a contract. Usually, if a buyer fails to get financing on a home-purchase deal, the buyer gets the earnest money back. I felt so bad for the builder and everyone else involved that I forfeited the $1k of earnest money and let the builder keep it for his troubles.

Until now, all the Ds of the Deal have had winners—buyers, sellers, realtors—all winners. In this one, though, Decline, there was no winner. The builder had to put a home he thought was already sold back on the market, wait to resell it, then wait to get paid.

Britney and I failed to receive the home we so desperately wanted. The builder's realtor failed to receive her commission.

While it was difficult to Decline that fabulous new home, the builder would soon resell it, the realtor would soon get a commission, and another family would be blessed with a great place to live. And who knows, for us, it may be a blessing in disguise for us, too.

## Ds of the Deal

That house may have pushed Britney and me over the edge financially, where we would lose money every month instead of coming out ahead.

Don't be afraid to Decline a deal when it is not in your best interest. Some deals Decline automatically, like if your financing isn't in order or if both parties can't come to terms, but on most deals you have to consciously Decline. It's not easy, but it's usually for the best.

Have you ever Declined a Deal? Have you ever been forced to back out of the Deal? How might Declining a Deal wind up being the best thing for you?

# D 13 - Depression

*Depression is an affliction so severe that it significantly restricts a person's ability to function fully, a crater in the mind so deep that no one can responsibly suggest it would surely go away if those victims would just square their shoulders and think more positively.*

**Jeffrey R. Holland**

Depression is an unfortunate thing that many people experience. I had a client/seller who had a series of things happen that caused him to be Depressed. First, his wife left then divorced him. Second, his adopted grandma passed away. Third, he had a disagreement with a neighbor who threatened to get a restraining order against him. All these things happened within a few months of each other, leaving this man in a Depressed state.

When his adopted grandmother passed away, she left him a nice house that he could either live in or sell.

## Ds of the Deal

Because he was Depressed, he decided to liquidate everything he owned, including this house. His plan was to sell everything and move to another state.

This home was a spacious 5,000-square-foot home, with an all-brick exterior, 5 bedrooms, 5 bathrooms, with a fully fenced 1-acre lot, and a 4-car garage.

To top it off, there was an enclosed four-seasons deck, and a mini-bar in the master bathroom.

If you saw it in person, you would agree this was a lot of house with some first-rate features. Rick, my Realtor partner, and I were, of course, this Depressed man's first choice when it came to listing this home to get it SOLD.

He told us he just wanted out of the house, that he was willing to take less, and wasn't

## Ds of the Deal

particularly worried about every nickel and dime of profit.

We priced the home accordingly, pricing it for a quick sale as our clients asked. We immediately got so much activity on the home, many calls and texts and emails about the property. We had a lot of in-person showings as well.

Neighbors of the listed property were also interested in purchasing the home. Needless to say, it was a frenzy.

At one point our client even said he would knock $50k off the price—almost a 20 percent discount—for a cash Deal that would close quickly. Since our client was Depressed and ready to move on with his life, he was willing to give a buyer a good Deal.

As fate would have it, we quickly got our client an offer he was comfortable with signing, and got under contract. A few weeks later, the seller received his cash, Rick and I got our commission, and the buyer got a great Deal on this fabulous, all-brick home on a 1-acre lot.

The transaction went smoothly because of the Depression that our client experienced, and everyone got what they wanted. It was another win-win-win situation, a win for the buyer, a win for seller, a win for Mike and Rick.

**Ds of the Deal**

Have you ever felt like this seller? Have you ever been Depressed and willing to take a hit or make a sacrifice just to be Done with the situation? Whether you have felt this way in the past or not, keep your eyes open for people who may be Depressed and need the solution only you can provide.

# D 14 - Drunk

*My definition of sobriety is to be in full control and not feel Drunk.*

**Spencer Matthews**

Have you ever seen someone or known of someone who did something that was so outrageous that you assumed they were Drunk or under the influence? What were they doing? Was it funny? Was it serious? Did they actually turn out to be Drunk?

Let me tell you about a real estate transaction where I was almost 100 percent certain that the buyers were Drunk or under the influence. First, it's important to know that a portion of my income is made through generating commissions. I generate commissions by helping people buy and sell real estate. I help solve people's problems. I get my buyers and sellers what they want.

There is one transaction in particular that really sticks out to me as a transaction where the

## Ds of the Deal

buying party may have been Drunk, or at least acting irrationally. I represented the seller in this transaction. I first listed the seller's home on the market. Unfortunately, this home was in extremely rough shape. It had been neglected, maintenance had been deferred, and there was a lingering smell of oil and curry throughout the whole house. There were some major concrete and foundation issues, too.

Among the imperfections, the hardwood floors were extremely worn. The carpet was matted and stained beyond cleaning. There were grease stains on the walls and holes in the drywall. The front porch concrete had sunk, and the rear wooden porch was rotting through. You get the gist, a home in need of extreme love, love that would cost big money. It was just trashed.

# Ds of the Deal

When I went to list the house for sale by putting it on all the realtor websites, I ran all my comparables, meaning all the houses that had recently sold in that area that had the same number of bedrooms and bathrooms and square footage.

After running my comparables and factoring in the current state of the home, I came up with a home value of about $160k, but that was a best-case scenario.

My sellers were not happy about that price, thinking the home was worth at least $200k. Despite the proof of my comparables, they were determined to list the home close to $200k, and threatened not to use me as realtor if I did not list it for that much. I didn't want to lose the potential listing. I wanted to earn the seller's business and take advantage of the potential to make a commission. I decided to list the home at the price the sellers wanted, which ended up being $210k.

Purely because of location, we had half dozen showings as soon as it hit the market. The feedback from every showing was the same: the home was in a great location but was extremely overpriced for the condition of the home. I was not surprised by this feedback, which gave me ammunition to throw at my seller showing that

# Ds of the Deal

the home was overpriced. My sellers remained adamant that they wouldn't list it for or take less than $210k, which made me a little discouraged. I had spent much time and effort listing and showing this home, many showings, which looked like it might go to waste.

After the home had been listed for about a week, we got a new showing, a couple who had recently moved to town and needed a house quickly. The potential buyer's realtor walked them through the house and they loved it, as is. I was extremely surprised. They said they would take the home, and were willing to pay $206k, just $4k less than the full list price.

I was so astounded I became a little apprehensive about the situation. I wanted to see proof of financing/proof of funds of these buyers, to make sure that they were, in fact, qualified to get a loan for the property.

To my surprise, this couple said they could pay almost half of the purchase price as a down payment, meaning that even if the home didn't appraise for the purchase price, it wouldn't matter because they were putting so much money as a down payment. This was literally a golden offer on a silver platter, and I am still shocked that the couple paid that much money for that house in that condition.

# Ds of the Deal

As you would expect, my sellers accepted this offer, and we officially started the home-selling process. In the back of my mind, I wondered what these buyers were thinking. I thought they must be Drunk or something, at least unfamiliar with property values in Springfield, Missouri.

To the surprise of us all, these buyers barely asked for any repairs on the home. Typically, when a buyer is purchasing a home, they get a home inspection and have a big list of items to fix before the Deal can close. This was not the case on this house. The buyers asked for a few reasonable things to be repaired, and not much else.

This Deal left my jaw dropped. Not only did we get almost $50k more than what the property was worth, we also got by without making many repairs. The day of closing came and everyone signed their documents transferring the home from my sellers into the hands of the new buyers. My sellers were overjoyed, of course, but, to my surprise, so were the buyers.

I still wonder what was going on inside the heads of the buyers. Were they Drunk? All I know is my sellers and I lucked out, the seller because they got a higher purchase price and me because a great commission was gained and another transaction closed.

## Ds of the Deal

Sometimes the right Deal just kind of stumbles in your lap, almost like a Drunk person would stumble in or out of a bar. You will see that as you further your business, become more high-functioning and more successful, that you may have a Drunk Deal stumble into your lap, benefiting you and your clients.

Keep your eyes open for the next Deal. Deals come in all shapes and sizes, and some come when you least expect it, like this Deal.

What can you do to keep your eyes open for the next Deal? Are you willing to make a conscious focus to always be attentive to potential Deals?

# D 15 - Demand

*I am like any other man. All I do is supply and demand.*

**Al Capone**

I can count on one hand the number of times I have paid what something is worth. Again, one of the best phrases you can apply to making a profit is, "you make your money when you buy." You always want to buy stuff for less, sometimes significantly less, than what it is worth.

The few times I can remember paying what something was worth are when I bought my 2019 Toyota Tacoma and drove it off of the lot, when I bought my Sig 9mm pistol, and when I bought a 32-unit apartment complex in my hometown.

Let's dive into that Deal with the apartment complex. If you know much about real estate investing, you know that apartment complexes are not often for sale. People who have apartment complexes love and hold onto them for dear life.

## Ds of the Deal

Apartment complexes are similar to the mini-storage facilities featured in *HUSTLE Then Repeat*.

People who own apartments and mini-storage facilities make such a good return, and have such a great investment, that there is usually no reason to sell. When you want to acquire an asset like a mini-storage facility or an apartment complex, you have to ask yourself, "why would they sell it to me?"

How can you get inside the owner's head or create a situation to talk them into selling this awesome asset for a decent price.

When Britney and I acquired our mini-storage facility, we were thrilled. It took offers on 29 different facilities before one of them stuck. We had an immense amount of time, effort, and cold calling invested before we saw any results. It was a similar ordeal when we bought our first apartment complex.

First, let me give you a little insight on our apartment complex. It has 32 units. There are 22 2-bedroom, 1-bathroom apartments and 10 1-bedroom, 1-bathroom apartments. The facility is spread out on almost an acre of property. There is a pool, a common area washer and dryer utility room, dozens of parking spaces, wide hallways for

## Ds of the Deal

easy movement of furniture, and porches or decks on just about all the units.

This apartment complex was located in a B+ area, definitely not the high end of town, but far from the low end. It is close to the Missouri State University campus, close to malls and shopping, and located convenient to many other businesses and major highways. The location was great for what Britney and I were looking for.

My stepfather, who had been in real estate for decades, had owned a 36-unit apartment complex in one of the crappiest, most drug-ridden, police-patrolled neighborhoods in all of Springfield.

I had grown up there, painting walls, tearing up carpet, evicting people, placing new tenants, and my personal favorite, picking up any coins I found. On average, I found from $3 to $5 dollars in change in every apartment we had to trash out or clean out after an eviction.

Finding that free money may have been one of the turning points when I started to value money, even nickels and pennies, more than ever.

## Ds of the Deal

In comparison to the old and crappy apartment complex my stepdad owned, our new 32-unit complex was a shining diamond.

Let's jump into our quest to purchase this apartment complex. After Britney and I had acquired about a dozen single-family rentals, plus the mini-storage facility, we realized that the next step for us was diversification in the form of an apartment complex. Part of this decision to tackle a bigger project came because I was hanging around people who were pretty well off and business-minded.

It seems like the more and more I was hanging out with these big-time investors, the better and better I became, and the bigger and bigger my dreams grew.

A few of my buddies were buying apartment complexes, and since I thought I had mastered the single-family game, I felt ready to acquire my own apartments.

The first apartment complex I took a stab at was an 19-unit facility for only $285k. That's only $15k per unit.

This first complex was totally in the hood, only two blocks from the crappy 36-unit facility my stepdad used to own, part of the drug-ridden, super sketchy side of town.

# Ds of the Deal

I kept telling myself "it's all about price," "it's all about price." If I could get it cheap enough, I wouldn't mind owning a property in the hood, and $15k per unit was definitely cheap enough for me to justify owning a Dumpy property.

I came across this facility through our local MLS realtor website. I saw this Deal pop up, and I kid you not, within 10 minutes it was already Pending. This meant they had already accepted an offer. I couldn't believe it. I literally watched it get put on the market and then sell 10 minutes later.

Feeling a little frustrated, I called the seller's realtor directly and asked him what the Deal was. He explained that this Deal had been so sweet they already had a buyer lined up before they put it on the market.

## Ds of the Deal

They only listed it to market the property as pending/sold to boost this realtor's sales numbers for the year. I realized I didn't even stand a chance from the start.

Even though I saw it pop up as active, it never really was. It was gone before I even knew it existed. That was kind of a bummer to me, but I was still determined to make a Deal happen with it. I continually called and texted the seller's realtor during the sale process of this 19-unit apartment complex, following up to see if there was any chance it might fall through so I could come pick up the pieces and buy it. I had no luck, as the property was sold without a hitch and no issues.

After that property sold, I reached out to the new owner through his real estate agent and made him an offer of $320k for the property, which would have provided a quick $35k profit for him without putting time or effort into it.

He declined my offer, but I let everyone know I would be a buyer in the future if anything changed on their end. That was the end of that Deal.

My second apartment endeavor came soon after. A friend of a friend put me in contact with a guy name Mark, who was known as a slumlord. Mark owned hundreds and hundreds of crappy

## Ds of the Deal

units on the sketchy side of town. Everybody knew Mark would buy anything, even if it was falling down and meth infested.

Mark's properties were all seriously run-down, needing roofs and other repairs because of long-deferred maintenance. He would buy a property, maybe fix it up once, and then rent it until the end of time without putting a dime back into it. You know these type of landlords from movies or you've met them in person.

Mark was that kind of guy, and he made a whole lot of money at the expense of his properties slowly deteriorating.

I asked Mark if he had any apartments he would sell. To my surprise, he said he had two complexes he would sell. Both were in the rundown downtown area, as you would expect from Mark. The roofs were old and weathered, almost caving in. The floors and subfloors were so up and down and wonky that you felt like you were riding on a roller coaster getting vertigo while walking through the units.

The old wood paneling made you feel like you were back in the 70s, and there were major electrical and HVAC/Central Heat and Cooling systems that needed major repairs.

## Ds of the Deal

There was a long list of cosmetic items that were sure to cost extreme amounts of money, including bathroom fixtures, ceiling rot, mold, active leaks, foundation repair, structural repair, and worst of all, the smell of smoke lingered throughout both complexes.

# Ds of the Deal

There were 22 units between the two complexes, both fairly accessible to downtown night life, the Brewing Company, and the MSU campus. The location was surprisingly acceptable, but their condition was horrible. I knew that so much money was needed to make these units livable, rentable, and marketable.

Mark was asking $725k for all 22 units. This put the price just under $33k per unit, which was very much on the high side for their condition.

I brought a partner into the situation, one of my investor buddies who owned a few apartment buildings. I walked him through the 22 units and asked my buddy to put some numbers together on what it would cost to make these properties livable. After many hours crunching numbers, he came up with a remodel cost of $800k.

Oh my goodness, that just threw me back in my seat.

That meant that after purchasing the properties and remodeling the units we would have more than $1.5 million invested.

Money is all relative, of course, and that might have been great margins if the property and the property rents could support it. In this case though, the property value and property rents would not support that figure. A million and a half

## Ds of the Deal

was hundreds of thousands of dollars more than the property would be worth even after being fixed up.

After all the work, after all was said and done, we would still be in the hole a few hundred thousand dollars. I made Mark the highest offer I could afford, which was $600k. Mark said $600k was a no-go, which honestly gave me a breath of relief, as I really felt I was overpaying even at $600k.

That Deal with Mark's 22 units fizzled out at that point. Now, I was partially torn. The first apartment Deal I had my eye on was too good of a Deal that got snatched up too quickly, and the second Deal I had my eye on was not good enough and never would be unless the asking price was adjusted. You'll find as you acquire assets and put Deals together, rarely is it ever the first try that works out.

That cheesy phrase we've heard all our lives is true: "If at first you don't succeed, try, try again."

After getting back up and brushing off the metaphorical dirt, I got back to work. I was scrolling through Facebook one day and saw that one of my investment buddies just posted that he was purchasing an apartment complex. I was

## Ds of the Deal

thrilled for him. I also knew this investor buddy to be a wholesaler, where he would sell off investment property AS IS without any fixing up or modifications.

After seeing him post about this 32-apartment complex he was about to acquire, I reached out and asked what the likelihood of him wanting to sell that 32-unit complex for a profit would be. He said the likelihood was very low, that it would be a good asset for him until the end of time. A little discouraged, I said okay and put that nice 32-unit apartment complex in the back of my mind.

I followed up with my investor friend every few weeks for two months to see if he was ready to make a Deal. I always follow up, always do my due diligence. After many times going back-and-forth between us, I finally got some headwind and we eventually struck a Deal. We agreed on a purchase price of about $36k per unit.

This is definitely on the higher end of what you want to spend on a 1- or 2-bedroom apartment unit. My saving grace was that almost all of the units were occupied, with only two vacancies.

This meant that almost all of the units were cash flowing, as well as in good condition. I was only going to have to come in and get 2 units

## Ds of the Deal

ready to rent as opposed to 32 units, like I would if they were all vacant.

At the end of the day, I felt I was paying top dollar for this apartment complex, and was kicking myself a little because of it. There was a small amount of fixing up to do, such as filling in the community pool with concrete—to lower my liability in the complex—and a few other maintenance odds and ends. The biggest kicker was that a handful of the rents were low. Since most people had been renting at the facility for an extended time, some of the people were grandfathered in with a lower rent. I knew that after all the rents were raised to market value, I would be cash flowing between $3k-$5k monthly, depending on the monthly maintenance cost, and making all my bills and mortgage on the property. All of this being taken into account, the updates and repairs I would need to do, as well as the rent raising that would need to take place immediately, I felt like I was definitely paying top dollar.

I can tell you why it was okay that Britney and I were paying top dollar in six letters: D-E-M-A-N-D. Demand. The Demand on a property like this was immense. There was literally nothing else like it listed for sale.

## Ds of the Deal

Like we saw with that first 19-unit complex I tried to make an offer on, the good complexes almost always sell before they hit the market, and there is very little room for negotiation on the purchase price. I took a step back and realized I was lucky to have an opportunity to purchase such a big asset with such great potential in such a great location.

Think back to the details we read at the start of this chapter about this 32-unit apartment complex. It was in a stellar location, with B+ tenants, in a price point that almost anyone could afford, and close to everything.

I checked all my real estate websites, including the MLS and others, and there was nothing like this 32-unit apartment complex out there.

## Ds of the Deal

As you know, with less supply comes more Demand. The less there are of some product or asset or property, the more the buyer is willing to pay for it.

After crunching the numbers—and checking my bank account to make sure I had enough funds for the 20 percent of purchase price down payment—we committed to buying the property.

The supply for a property like this was zero and the Demand was high.

Even though I was paying top dollar, I knew I could list it for sale and have people fighting over it at the price I bought it for, simply because there is more Demand for apartment buildings because they are more scarce.

When it comes to apartment buildings, it seems like that is almost always the case. The factor of supply and Demand works in the favor of an apartment seller.

Although Britney and I were ecstatic about this new apartment complex, this story about Demand is also a win for the seller, because even at the price he sold me the apartment complex, he still made a few hundred thousand dollars in profit by wholesaling the property to us.

## Ds of the Deal

Does that make sense? He bought it lower, sold it to us for higher, and everyone was a winner. He made his money on the property, and Britney and I got a great asset that would soon cash flow.

Some of the rents were raised even before Britney and I closed on the 32 units. We were already on our way to cash flow and benefit from this property.

Just between us, although we bought this apartment complex in a time where there was less supply and more Demand, I still feel like we purchased a few hundred thousand dollars of equity. This complex will continue to appreciate and become worth more and more with every passing year.

The best part about this whole transaction was that the same loan officer who gave us our very first loan years before gave us the loan on this million-dollar apartment complex.

In a way, we felt our Deals were coming full circle. Carol, who originally helped us get started on the loan aspect of our rental property journey, had just loaned Britney and me more than 10 times the money she did on our first loan just a few years prior.

## Ds of the Deal

Relationships are very important when it comes to lending and putting Deals together. Having good relationships in business is mutually beneficial to all parties involved. Our relationship with Carol the lender got us a great Deal on the loan for this 32-unit apartment complex.

Our relationship with my investor buddy got us the opportunity to purchase this 32-unit apartment complex.

This is a perfect example of the fact that the *HUSTLE Then Repeat* and *Ds of the Deal* principles come full circle and uplift each other. Not in my wildest dreams did I think my wife and I would have a million-dollar apartment complex before

## Ds of the Deal

age 23, during a global pandemic, no less. That seems about as far-fetched and out of the ordinary as you or I can imagine.

What's a goal you can create today that seems far-fetched? How excited would you be if you attained that goal? How far would you go or how much are you willing to give to get what you truly desire and deserve?

Have you been on one side of the supply/Demand situation in the past? I promise that as you keep your eyes open for the Ds of the Deal, you will find the Deals that you so greatly desire, whether it be in real estate, vehicles, technology, building materials, or anything else.

The Ds of the Deal are everywhere. You just need to keep your eyes open for them.

# D 16 - Desire

*What you lack in talent can be made up with desire, Hustle, and giving 110 percent all the time.*

**Don Zimmer**

What do you desire? We all have Desires, whether we recognize them or not. Some of our Desires are subconscious, meaning we don't really know they are our Desires until we pay more attention. Other Desires can be apparent in our daily life and in our daily thought process. For example, someone who consciously Desires a healthier lifestyle will make an added effort to eat healthy and exercise, as opposed to someone who may subconsciously want better health without doing anything about it. Our Desires shape our decisions. Our decisions shape our life. If your Desires are either subconsciously or consciously negative, then negativity is more than likely what you will receive. If your Desires, conscious or subconscious, are positive, it is much more likely

## Ds of the Deal

that you will receive positive results throughout your life.

Let me tell you about a story where Desires definitely came into play. The first Desire of the story is the Desire I had to trade Britney's 2011 Chevy Equinox LT FWD Automatic Transmission SUV for a piece of property.

Britney's car only had 115k miles, and had been treated extremely well by Britney. If you know Britney, she drives like a grandma 95 percent of the time.

The other 5 percent consists of her pure road rage, but the majority of miles that Britney put on this awesome little SUV were easy-going miles.

We received this Equinox as a wedding present when we came home from our ministry trips and got married, a gift from Britney's dad. This is the same Dad who had sold me a blue convertible BMW in high school, and created my first monthly debt payment. This time, he gave us the vehicle outright, a very generous move.

Britney drove the car for two and a half years, when we realized we would need something bigger since we planned on growing our family soon. As you know, monthly payments on newer, nicer cars don't come cheap. We could pay cash for a new car, but our money makes more money

# Ds of the Deal

when invested in real estate. We knew if we did get a new car we would have to finance the purchase and have a steep monthly payment, which we didn't have with the Equinox.

Taking all this into account, I told Britney that if we could trade her car for an asset that would generate $300 or more a month, we could justify getting her a new car with a $300 car payment. Britney graciously agreed to let me fulfill my Desire to trade her car for a piece of property. As we learned in *HUSTLE Then Repeat*, any deal is possible if you put your mind to it and give 110 percent into working the deal.

I started the process of trading Britney's car by getting on the MLS realtor website to see what kind of low-priced houses were on the market. Out of the almost 1,000 properties listed in my MLS geographical area, only 3 fit the potential price range of my wife's car, $5k-$15k. I called all 3 listing realtors in that low price range and presented the awesome idea of trading my wife's reliable SUV for the crappy houses they had listed for sale. All three presented my out-of-the-ordinary offer to their sellers, and all three rejected it. One of the realtors even made fun of me. He said his seller would take the car on trade, and went so far as to ask me to get the car detailed. While on my way to get the car detailed,

## Ds of the Deal

I called the realtor, who laughed and said he had been "kidding" the whole time.

Having exhausted the MLS market, I decided to try the next best thing, Facebook Marketplace. Many things can be sold on Facebook Marketplace, including cars, cell phones, bicycles, motorcycles, and houses. After scouring Facebook Marketplace for a potential property, I finally found a 3-bedroom, 1-bath home listed for $25k. This home was in a rough area, as most $25k houses tend to be.

The seller was a retiring pastor who was selling his own little rental property. I sent him pictures and information about my wife's car. He said he was willing to take it on trade, with one condition: he wanted $15k cash added on our end. I wasn't Desirous to put that kind of money on my end of the deal, not for a crappy house. I countered with $6k plus Britney's car. He countered with $10k plus the car for the crappy house. Thinking the price was too high for us, I walked away from the deal.

A few weeks later, I Desired to give that house another shot. Lo and behold, the house had sold to someone else. I had hesitated and lost the deal, which made me unhappy. I had been a little too stingy and should have settled on the $10k

## Ds of the Deal

plus the car for that crappy house. Feeling the regret, I set out to find another property.

A few more weeks went by and I couldn't find anything priced low enough to equal the value of Britney's car. One night, as I was going to bed, I checked the new property listings on the MLS website. To my surprise, I saw a nice lot with a shop building for only $22.9k. Britney's car was only worth $7,000 at best, but I went ahead and offered Britney's car as trade for that little lot with the shop building. Not to my surprise, the seller said the value of Britney's car was too low for them to consider a trade. The seller was open to a trade, though, for anything with value, which I thought was a good sign. I decided to offer my 2017 Suzuki DR 200S Enduro Motorcycle, valued at $4k, as part of the trade.

Although the seller saw the value of the bike, he didn't know how to ride a motorcycle and did not Desire something he couldn't readily use. After going back-and-forth for a few weeks, I realized the seller of this lot and shop building wanted to purchase an even bigger property with an even bigger shop building on it. His construction business was booming, so much that he needed something bigger. What a happy problem to have, needing a bigger building and a bigger lot because your business is doing so well.

## Ds of the Deal

I was happy for the seller, who Desired something bigger and better to keep his business going. That Desire, I believe, is the reason he was even remotely thinking about a trade for a car.

Except for the 3-bedroom, 1- bathroom seller, the other sellers I had talked to had no Desire to take an SUV as trade for a property. The Desire was there in this seller to sell.

The Desire was in Britney and me to trade the car. Britney Desired a bigger and better car with three rows and captain seats to support our many children we would soon have coming down the pipeline. I Desired to not have to pay for that new car by having an asset that would cash flow at least $300 monthly.

We all had our Desires in this situation, the seller's Desire to sell, Britney's Desire for the new car, and my Desire to trade her current car for a cash-flowing asset. All of our Desires were there, and all in line with each other.

After a few more weeks of back-and-forth through the seller's realtor, we struck an agreement. It was going to take $10k and Britney's $7k SUV trade to purchase this lot with a shop building on it. Despite having to put a little cash on our end, I was ecstatic to yet again trade a vehicle for more real estate.

## Ds of the Deal

With hindsight, I would have much preferred to put $10k and Britney's car toward that 3-bedroom, 1-bathroom house, but we all make mistakes. I had a decent enough deal in front of me, trading the car and some cash for this lot that would easily rent for $395 a month.

Just one day after we finalized the deal, one day after closing, we were offered $30k for this lot with shop building on it. What a day, and what a quick way to make $13k profit if we had Desired to unload the property.

Britney was equally ecstatic with this amazing trade of a vehicle for real estate. She was so happy because that meant one thing: she got a new car with a monthly payment that would soon be canceled out by the rent of the new property we were trading for.

## Ds of the Deal

After looking at a few cars, one stuck out to Britney better than the rest, a 2016 Lincoln Navigator 4x4 SUV with all the luxuries that come with owning a Lincoln.

This car had the V-6 turbo eco-boost engine, as well as a massive sunroof, with a big touchscreen and powerful audio system, blind spot monitors, and—best of all—heated and cooled seats.

It wasn't until a few days after the purchase that we realized that not only the front seats were heated, but the seats in the middle row were heated, too.

We were overjoyed to have such a luxurious vehicle, where even our passengers could have their butts warm.

Needless to say, it was a win-win for everybody. Britney's Desire for a new car was met, my Desire to acquire new assets was met, and the seller's

Desire to move up from his little property with the storage building on it was met.

## Ds of the Deal

You will see, as you put Deals together in your business and throughout your life, that Desires are what really drive people. Find the Desire in your customer or client, and by doing so you will become their solution.

What do you Desire? Do you have different Desires in relation to different parts of your life? What is your biggest business Desire? What is your biggest personal Desire?

Find your Desires and recognize them, because whether you like it or not, they are a major motivation in your life.

**Ds of the Deal**

**Ds of the Deal** ─────────────

# D 17 - Dirtbag (Don't Be One)

*An unpleasant person who has done something dishonest or unacceptable.*

**Cambridge Dictionary**

During the beginning stages of writing this book, the wife of one of my friends overheard the general principles of this book and things I planned to discuss.

Her response was different, unexpected. Instead of the praise I am used to when mentioning my books and business principles, she called me a Dirtbag. Ouch!

That got me thinking. I want to make the point, to stress the point, that we shouldn't be Dirtbags. Every human being deserves respect and the best treatment possible.

The Golden Rule applies, to treat others as you want to be treated. You may think taking

## Ds of the Deal

advantage of someone is good only if it gets you personal gain, but that's not really good.

All of my Deals have had the full consent of everyone involved, and every situation has resulted in win-wins. I only make a Deal if it's mutually beneficial to everyone involved.

So, don't be a Dirtbag. Being a Dirtbag is NOT one of the Ds of the Deal.

# D 18 - Ds of the Deal Capital

*In order to access private capital, you have to provide competitive return on investment. In order to give competitive returns to investors, you've got to operate on a profitable basis and be thinking of yourself as a business.*

**Pierre Omidyar**

Don't know where to start? Need help taking the first steps investing in the world of real estate?

Britney and I have established a way for you to get a GUARANTEED RETURN on your money, while learning how to invest in real estate in the process.

We call it Deal Capital, a way for you to receive up to 10 percent GUARANTEED ANNUAL RETURN on your money. The way this works is simple, and it's been proven time and time again.

# Ds of the Deal

You contribute money to Deal Capital, and your money goes toward Britney's and my next investment property. Britney and I pay you 10 percent ANNUAL INTEREST RETURN for as long as you like, the term agreed to by both parties up front.

At the end of your term, you get 100 percent of your money returned to you. Many people have loaned money to our investment projects, and every single one has profited and left happier and more wealthy.

One story in particular is highlighted in *HUSTLE Then Repeat*. An older couple wanted to make a guaranteed investment with money that was just sitting in their bank account, doing nothing for them.

They loaned Britney and me $12k to go toward our most recent investment project. We paid this couple %/Interest on their money for almost two years, at which point we paid them off completely.

Both parties were thrilled, the older couple with the money they had made by doing nothing other than loaning us money, Britney and I because of the progress we made with these extra funds.

**Ds of the Deal** ─────────

Reach out to us through our website McgeeBowman@murney.com to get more information and get enrolled in this high-return investment group.

# Final Deal

*You have the drive, you have the motivation. That's one reason you are reading this book. Keep it handy and reread it often. Now put down the book and get to work.*

**Mike Bowman**

Here's something that can help.

You can subscribe to public records that keep track of Deaths, Divorces, Debts (foreclosures) and other situations that might lead a seller to sell an asset to you at a Discounted price and be happy for the opportunity.

A system we have used in the past is a website called *offrs.com*.

For only $900, we got public information on thousands of people who may need help selling assets at a mutually beneficial price.

**Ds of the Deal**

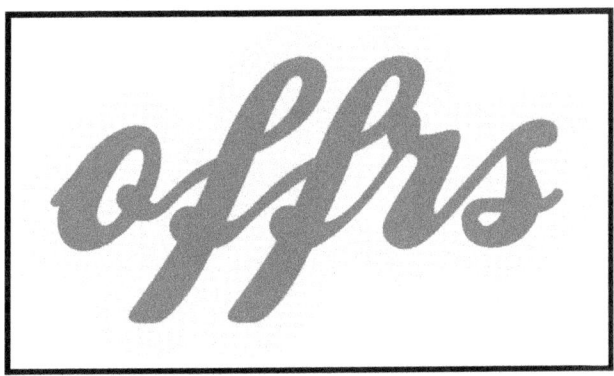

Feel free to check out *offrs.com* for information that may lead you to potential great Deals.

Keep in mind, although this information is somewhat personal, it is all public record and can be accessed by anyone, including you if you know where to look.

**Ds of the Deal**

May you and your family find all of the good Deals that you can actively handle, and may God bless you.

# Leave a Review

If you found this book useful or otherwise enjoyable, tell your family, friends, and coworkers. That's what Facebook, Twitter, and Instagram are for, right?

Please follow this link to leave a review on Amazon. I will read and consider what you say, because I want to provide the best books I can. Your input helps.

Review *Ds of the Deal* at this link:

https://amzn.to/2IHJPrI

Thank you again for buying this book. Now, show us what you can do when you *HUSTLE* using *The Ds of the Deal*.

**Ds of the Deal**

*"Britney got a new car with a monthly payment that would soon be canceled out by the rent of the new property we were trading for."*